Here's to Making it Count

By Heidi Passalacqua

SHIRES PRESS

4869 Main Street
P.O. Box 2200
Manchester Center, VT 05255
www.northshire.com

Here's to Making it Count
©2015 by Heidi Passalacqua

ISBN: 978-1-60571-244-4

Printed in the United States of America

Special Thanks

Dear Lord God, I never thought I would write a book. I didn't start out in my life having a belief in you, but in my life, it was evident-and folks you will see if you look beyond this page-that you had a plan for me. Thank you for giving me guidance, showing me forgiveness and helping me grow within you. Thank you for granting me courage, building resilience and patience and being able to help me find the ability to share my wisdom in this journey. You are my compass, my True North. I pray others will find you in my words.

I have quite an extensive family now and every one of them I am thankful to for helping me in this work. I appreciate your encouragement. Sometimes your tough love was needed in telling me to "make the most of it". It pushed me to go beyond my limit, to believe I could accomplish this.

Bill, you have been the conduit always believing that this "will get done", well finally it has.

Vicki your "debt" is paid. Your selfless hours you spent in front of the computer looking up publishers, editing, editors, books, pushing me to believe in myself telling me to "get a professional editor"(!), has been such a Godsend. This was our work together. I so value your time, talent and friendship. You are a gem, another gift I am grateful that God opened for me to see.

When people say "it takes a village "it really does. In this case a town, the community of Northfield and Norwich. The community is an unbelievable place which surrounds its people in good times and in bad. When you share your burdens they are there for you. They have always been "there" for me and my family.

Everyone has a story to tell. I hope my story will help others know that there is hope, that there is a way.

Nestled in the heart of central Vermont, there is a small military school called Norwich University. The corps of cadets there has as part of its creed and guiding values: "I believe that the cardinal virtues of the individual are courage, honor, temperance and wisdom; and that the true measure of success is service rendered – to God, to country and to Mankind."

Courage

"To stand firm in your convictions
in the face of opposition or adversity"

I felt as though I was at the bottom of a pool. I could see the blue sky above me, with the light shining so brightly up on the surface. The water felt cold, bone-chilling. I was stuck at the bottom of the pool and I had a choice to make. I could take my feet, push with all my might, thrusting my body upward towards that beautiful, perfectly blue sky, filled with warmth and comfort and renewing air. Or I could allow my lungs to fill with the cold water and let the blackness and darkness encircle me and drown. I could push off the floor, releasing that terrible burden, giving up on living, and replacing it with feeling weightless, rising faster to the surface. Having the feeling, the longing for that first, spontaneous, yet life-renewing breath. Then when breaking the surface of that cold darkness and opening my lungs to the air, seeing the sky, the feeling of the awesome reward of relief and joy is so renewing.

That feeling for the most part is life-renewing, hopeful, invigorating. There have been times, though, when I have felt like I couldn't get out from under the water. The struggle took longer; the kick seemed harder, more strenuous. There was a panic of never reaching that breath of air and thinking I would drown for sure. I have felt that way three distinct times in my life. Reaching the surface has been inspirational, courageous, and forgiving. I haven't always felt I had the kick in me. Developing the wisdom and patience has been difficult and has been a decades-long process. It was difficult until I made a choice. I would like to share the journey.

I was in bed, emotionally tired after the day and physically tired from night skiing with the town Outing Club. My family and friends had strongly suggested that my sister and I get away from the hospital, home, and daily routine.

My mom had been in the hospital for two weeks at that point. She was in intensive care after collapsing one morning with internal bleeding. She was an alcoholic; I had known for some time. At age sixteen, I was the adult child of an alcoholic parent, living in Vermont, with a father stationed in Germany. The morning she headed to the hospital, she was up unusually early. I rose every morning to feed the horses around 5:30 a.m. so I could then get back to the house in time to shower and catch the 7:10 bus during the week. I had asked her why she was up so early and she said a friend down the road was taking her to the hospital. When she told me she was bleeding internally, I asked her how she knew and she answered she "just did."

We had a blast, my first time skiing at night. It was invigorating and for a time I forgot that I was the oldest; that at sixteen, I was the adult and that I had responsibilities beyond my comprehension awaiting me. I guess I wasn't only tired: I was exhausted. Settling into bed, I fell asleep fast and began to dream.

In this dream, my mother was in my room talking to me. She was standing at the foot of my bed, only she wasn't standing on the floor; she sort of hovered to the right of the corner, about the level of the bed. Almost like she was standing on my bed, but just a few inches above it. She was telling me that she was sorry for all the trouble, sorry for blaming me for her behavior, but it was time for her to go and she knew I would take care of everything – I already had. At the other side of my bed was a feeling of heat and it appeared as a red light. I had the sense that it was danger. I kept looking at it and trying to talk to my mother, but I couldn't speak. My mother said I would be safe and said that it was time for her to go. I woke up startled, but at peace. It was later I learned the exact time my mother had visited me and died, crossing over into another world. My father came in about an hour later, waking me to tell me that my mother had passed away, but I told him I already knew. I was now the adult child of an alcoholic; a deceased alcoholic.

My mother and father met on Long Island. In understanding my father, it is important to understand where he came from. He immigrated from Germany in about 1953 after growing up in war-torn Germany and Holland. From what I have gleaned from my father, he essentially grew up in Holland with his Taunta (Aunt) Freida and his Dutch uncle. My dad has two older brothers.

My mother, also of German descent, grew up in the family insurance business. My parents first met in elementary school, but didn't actually connect until my father's mother, (my "Nana") took him to get insurance for a car, while he was attending

Norwich University in Northfield, Vermont. My mother drove an Alpine Sunbeam convertible and my Nana told my dad to go for a ride. My mother asked my father if he wanted to drive her car and my dad said "yes," even though he didn't know how to drive a stick shift well. As my dad says now, she probably wished she hadn't, as they struggled – jerking forward and backward around the block with my dad grinding the gears. From then on, under the very controlling watch of my Nana, my parents dated. It was while attending Norwich that the Northfield connection began. My dad had lost his father to cancer shortly after moving to the United States, when he was only fourteen. Dad became very close with the Philosophy, Religion, and Fine Arts professor at school. He was also a Catholic monsignor and the university chaplain at Norwich. He adored my mother and after he graduated, my parents married. Under my Opa's (my grandfather's) advisement, my dad attended and received his doctorate at Georgetown University. He was also in the army and within a few months of my birth he deployed to Vietnam. My mother and I lived with my Opa in Vermont, attending many functions at Norwich, as the president of the university and his wife took us under their wing.

After my father returned, we were stationed at West Point, where he taught, and where my sister Elena was born. We travelled frequently to Vermont during our time in New York.

Many current and retired generals that my father mentored now recall babysitting my sister and me.

We lived in New York, California, Kansas, and Virginia before my dad was scheduled to deploy to Germany for at least four years. Opa had since passed away and our family decided to do what they called a "split operation." My mother, sister, and I would live in Vermont, while my father would head to Germany. My mother felt strongly that Elena and I should start and finish high school in the same place and it appeared that this would not happen if we went to Germany. So we moved the horses and dogs to Vermont in May of 1981.

My mom re-established relationships she had begun while she and I had lived in Vermont before. The university president had since retired and moved on. It was a different campus and I had the perception that unless you worked there, or had a parent that worked there, you were not welcome.

I initially didn't want to be welcomed either. I was entering eighth grade. I was happy in Virginia and being a teenager there was much easier, as there was plenty to do. My mother told me to make the most of it, since I wasn't going anywhere. An incident during Memorial Day and the interment of my Opa (he passed away in the winter but could not be buried then) helped me to begin my "root-making." We had a St. Bernard named Brandy and he was only about a year old. He was about 130 pounds and still growing. During the reception after the burial,

Brandy took off up the road. No one actually noticed him take off; we just knew he was missing when dinner came. Since he NEVER missed a meal, we suspected a problem. We drove around looking for him that evening and for a couple of days, posting "missing/lost" signs up all over town. On the hill we lived on, I got dropped off on a long driveway leading to a log cabin house. There was a young lady lying out on the lawn in her bathing suit with an aluminum foil reflective blanket for added heat. Her name was Sara. She hadn't seen Brandy, but I found out she was in the same grade I was. She offered to show me around.

A few days went by. Our family was sitting out on the porch, which overlooked the driveway as well as the road. The house had a cantilevered staircase made of railroad ties leading up to where we sat. I looked out on the almost setting sun to see Brandy walking very slowly up the driveway. I yelled and pointed, "He's back!" My dad, who up to now had thought Brandy was a goner, ran to him and the two shared a big bear-like hug. It was then that I noticed two red splotches on the front of Brandy's chest and told my dad it looked like he had been shot. Brandy was wet up to his chest. My dad quickly loaded him into the Subaru, told my mom to call the vet, and they were on their way.

Brandy was lucky to be alive. He had in fact taken two bullets at close range from a 22-caliber gun. From where the bullets entered, the vet figured he had to have been sitting down when he was shot. One bullet was inoperable and would remain in his tissue; the other could not be located. The vet also noted Brandy had been shot in the snout and the bullet had ricocheted off of one of his teeth, or Brandy had swallowed it. Anyway, he guessed that once Brandy had been shot he had gone and laid in a cold mountain stream, slowing his bleeding lowering his temperature, and starting the healing process. After a few weeks he was back to normal. We never did find who shot our dog. Brandy didn't trust some men for several years. Some he seemed fine with; with others he would get this look like something out of Stephen King's book *Cujo* and I recall one man seeing the inside of Brandy's mouth when he entered unannounced into our home.

My mom visited my dad in Germany during the next few years, with people my parents knew taking care of my sister and me so we could continue school schedules and take care of the horses. Shortly before my mother died, she had been planning to go to Europe to a center that specialized in the treatment of substance abuse. A very good friend and neighbor of my parents had gone several years before and was recovering. My mother was told to continue to drink until she entered the hospital. Apparently with extreme alcoholism individuals shouldn't attempt withdrawal on their own, but should enter a treatment center for help to avoid the serious complications during the detoxification that happens. Norma, our neighbor had had such success that my mother was very hopeful and being that my father was in Germany this seemed logical. When my mother tried to "detox" on her own her body simply went into shock. Years later, I learned her liver, kidneys and stomach were in such bad shape she just didn't have much of a chance. I just don't have any idea of "why" she decided to stop on her own and do that to herself. It must have been awful to go through.

Growing up, I questioned whether or not my mom was an alcoholic. I remember a few times while we were switching duty stations, she ended up in the hospital. This happened once while we were visiting my grandmother in Florida and again when we were on vacation in California camping in Eureka. I recall the hospital admissions were to treat the "ulcers" my mother had. She was an awful eater and she smoked and drank. When we lived in Kansas, my father once tossed a number of large bottles of vodka and rum out our second-story window, smashing them to bits on our driveway below.

As I got older and started learning more about the effects of alcohol, I started questioning my mother. I never saw her drink at home, but recall late at night hearing the sound of a kitchen cabinet, where my mom stored the liquor, popping when she would open it. I could see into the kitchen from my room and would see my mom pour liquor into a cup. I never really looked at her as an alcoholic, because to me she didn't look like an alcoholic. She didn't go out, she always took care of us with our lunches made, dinner made, and the house was always clean – super clean. She was always ready for people when they dropped over. She loved to entertain. I recall there were many parties while I was growing up. My mother was a gourmet cook. She hosted many officers' parties with themed cooking. She even made hotdogs into a gourmet meal. She mentored families. She volunteered at many different things in all the various places when we lived on base. When we moved to Vermont, my mom worked with the police. She was a member of the Ladies Reading Circle, which provided some re-connections from the previous time we had lived in Vermont. My friends would "run away" to our house and my mother continued to mentor them. Our house felt very comfortable.

What I don't remember is my mom coming to any of my activities or games when I played soccer or softball. Then, when I turned fifteen, I got my driver's permit. My mother, sister, and I would go to a local restaurant every Friday night. On one of the nights in the winter, my mom had had what I felt was too much to drink. As we were leaving, I asked if I could drive. My mother said no and I confronted her, telling her my suspicions. Even though she wasn't slurring her words or staggering, I just thought she was drunk. We argued and I got in the car in the passenger's seat. My sister got in the back. Coming up our hill, about a mile from the main road on the snow-covered drive, my mother turned her head to me and said "You want to drive, DRIVE." She let go of the steering wheel, keeping her foot on the gas. I couldn't react quickly enough even to understand what she was doing, because she hadn't stopped and was still in the driver's seat. We veered off the road into a drainage ditch. From then on, I didn't go to the restaurant on Friday nights with my mother and sister. I wrote my dad a letter that he still has to this day, telling him that mom was an alcoholic.

The town I lived in kicked in and basically took over. It was a wonderful community of about five thousand people. Being a teen who wanted nothing to do with my mother's drinking habit, I had gotten involved in every event I could. I was almost seventeen and struggling with getting ready for college. For the past couple of years I hadn't really been a teen, I'd been a mother to an alcoholic and a parent to my younger sister.

Initially a young couple, Jack and Jodi, moved in to help us transition. My father and mother knew Jack through my Opa. Jack and his wife, Jodi, would frequently come and stay with us when my mother traveled to Germany. My father would go back to Germany and then would move to Maryland during his first few months away. Also moving in were two Norwich University students, who were student-teachers at Northfield High School. They were very close to my mother and had been around a lot more recently, almost sensing the increased need for some "big brothers."

These two big brothers, named Gary and Ed, were members of Skull and Swords, a secret honor society from Norwich in which my Opa had been their mentor/advisor. After his death, their members (of which there were no fewer than six and no more than eight chosen each year) helped my mom accomplish chores around the house that neither my sister nor I could do. They helped by putting wood up for our huge furnace, mending fences, and horse-related tasks. In return, my mother enjoyed cooking for them and their company. She would make meals for all eight of them.

There were certain times of the year when my mother would get phone calls and would then casually go and shut the curtains of the large picture windows facing our road. The curtains were heavy and really kept sound out. These were truly the only times I remember those very heavy thick curtains being closed. It was usually in the spring. Shortly after the "closing of the curtains," usually in April, my mother, sister, and I would be invited to a parade beginning Junior Weekend at Norwich. Eight new rising seniors would be "tapped in" during the ceremony at the parade. Norwich printed the ceremony with their names and a description of what the parade represented, calling the Skull and Swords parade "the greatest honor bestowed upon a cadet." Elena and I were called "little sisters." It was nice to know that I had big brothers who would look out for us.

During this time, humor was used a lot to help assuage our grief. Jodi ran a tight ship. We all had chores to accomplish. Ed and Gary would team up with my sister or me and sometimes we would cook or clean. Ed and Gary made us laugh and then the combination of Jodi and Jack would have us on the floor sometimes. After several months, Ed and Gary were graduating and Jack and Jodi were planning to move back down the hill to their home. Elena started having a more difficult time, grieving again with Ed and Gary leaving. She needed to be told when to eat, sleep, go to the bathroom, and go to school. So she went down to live with Jack and Jodi. My father announced he would be getting remarried to Debbie, a woman he had known from when he was in Virginia (before he moved to Germany. My mother had mentioned that she had actually met Debbie in Germany as my sister shared years later that Debbie had moved there also). Because he wasn't in Vermont full time he would search for someone who would come and live with us and care for the horses rather than try to get rid of them all. I'm grateful my Dad didn't take my sister and me back to Germany or to Maryland which he could have done and to any other duty station. Some of our family on my mother's side urged him to take us, but we had lost our mother, we were in our home setting, and we would carry on as my mother had often said "make the most of it".

By the grace of God and the community I survived, went on to college, and graduated with a nursing degree. I left Vermont and moved to Rhode Island for a short time. While studying for my boards, I worked with children, newborn to two years of age, and I also worked as a nanny. I absolutely loved the children I encountered on the third floor of the Potter Building. In a short time I had seen quite a bit regarding childhood illness, disease, and death. I saw sorrow, pain, guilt, joy, attitude, and hope all in action with the nurses, the families, and the children. After working nights (let me add that I am not a night person), I ended up becoming ill with mononucleosis and decided that since the floor could not offer me a day or evening position, I would move back to Vermont. There, I quickly got a position working in home health. The position involved providing nursing care in family homes.

Working as a visiting nurse, it was easy for me to submerge myself in the pain and needs of others. I chose pediatric homecare because it is and has been a very dear thing to me. So many families needed me. One of the first clients I was assigned to made it necessary to travel ninety miles from home and I was placed again in a challenging home of a child who was expected to die. My assignment was basically to go home with the family and help this infant, born prematurely at twenty-four weeks, to go home with her family to die. The family, who lived in the mountains one and a half hours from the medical center, would have little opportunity to get to the center if anything happened to her. So, my job was to train other nurses to do shifts of caring for this little one, while trying not to interfere with the rest of the family. Well, it was difficult not to get involved. The mother and father, both Christians, were very endearing, pleasant, and welcoming. They were frightened of all the machines and of what to expect. When a child with so many special needs comes home from a hospital, where everything is right there, it can be very technical and overwhelming. You want the family to understand the machines that help their daughter to breathe; you want them to know how to change the tubing, change the tracheal cannula, change oxygen, and monitor weight, output, and intake, all very challenging things. Their daughter was a true miracle who touched so many lives. She showed those doctors at the medical center that she was a survivor. She was born between twenty-four and twenty-five weeks' gestation, just six short months in the womb. Her lungs had not developed and that was why she needed the continuous oxygen and pressure machine (called a CPAP machine) to help inflate her tiny little lungs. Then she would breathe out on her own.

Because of the distance of my trip and the fact that her care was so detailed, nurses who thought homecare was easy did not last long. They would actually come to orient for one shift, stay, and then call the scheduler and tell them they were quitting. That would mean either my supervisor or I would have to stay overnight or shift twelve hours on and twelve hours off between the two of us for a few days at a time.

After months of survival for this little one and a decrease in nursing hours, I was home and on call. The call came after a dream I was having of her: she was gasping for life and at the same time she was giggling at her mom and dad. The call, at 3 a.m., was that my patient's tracheotomy cannula had popped out and the doctor who came and did a house call could not get the tracheal tube back in. The family decided not to put their little girl through any more pain, so they refused to transport her to the local hospital. They were basically calling me to tell me their daughter was dying and to take my time coming up to make the "death in the home call." Well, when I arrived three hours later, wasn't I amazed at the glory of God's little miracle to find that precious angel quite alive, not in any pain, and giggling. She simply did not like that tracheotomy tube or the tubes in her way anymore. Well, as soon as she "ex-tubated" herself, it was easy to get nurses to come help. She didn't need the CPAP machine anymore, only oxygen. It was also very easy to accept positions with a warm, caring, loving family. I learned the most about hope and God's incredible divine nature and love in this home. I was no longer needed in their home other than to do "supervisory visits" and assessment visits. Years later, I learned that the little girl died of a respiratory virus. I imagine she is looking down and giggling at all of us.

I was also working with a single mother, who at age forty-two delivered a post-term baby boy with cerebral palsy. This little one had frequent seizures and often cried the entire shift of twelve to fifteen hours. The mother needed a nurse to care for her son, for help and for respite, so she could return to work. Her fight was with everyone, because according to her "the doctor should have induced her earlier; instead they took her baby (by C-section)." In her opinion, she did not give birth; she was violated. Then all of a sudden her independent private life gave way to relying on nurses to care for her son in her home – which meant no privacy for her. Now, when I say *forced* I really don't mean that. She accepted us into the home because she needed us, but we were definitely a hindrance sometimes. For her it would have been nice to come home from work and be able just to visit with her baby, eat in peace, sit, and watch the news. Many times she would be exhausted from working and since her son was so disabled, he would be "whining"/high pitched crying when she left and several hours later she would come home and he would be doing the same thing.

Her other fight was with Medicaid over the "decreasing nursing hours," As I mentioned before, the state would pay for twenty-four-hour care for a few days, then twenty-two hours for a week or two, then twenty for two weeks, decreasing gradually with the goal of only having to do nursing assessments a couple of times a month. Well, for many families this was difficult.

Sometimes the children would get worse (in which case they might be re-hospitalized and the hours would start all over). The other was that being nurses, used to doing everything for the patients and families in hospitals, we often took over all care during their shifts and then when it was time to decrease hours the families still had no idea what to do or how to cope. This has gotten better, but it is still difficult. Well, many a night I spent with this family, sometimes ending up in the ER of the hospital with the child having a very bad seizure or the gastric tube in the child's stomach coming out and me not being able to reinsert it.

I also learned a great deal with this family. I learned respect for a single parent; I learned the psychiatric reason why parents "snap" when their children have colic. Believe me; it is not easy to hear a baby cry/whine twenty hours of the day and feel unable to stop the crying or provide comfort, no matter what you try.

After my return to Vermont, other than work, I was not a big social butterfly. I had had some relationships, but had come home to Vermont with no intentions or ideas. When I was home, I spent time with Susan, the barn manager of my father's horse farm. It was in March of 1991 when Susan and I needed to begin the workouts for the show season ahead and to be in shape for the three to six students who needed instruction and transportation to show my father's horses.

"I know that all I do is work, but there just isn't anything for me right now, after breaking up with Clark," I stated to Susan one day.

"Yes, but you know what? You need a social life. You need to kick back and have some fun other than working or you will make yourself sick." Susan said this as she pulled on spandex pants in the barn apartment of the stables. "I'm telling you, love will happen when you least expect it."

She finished getting ready and we got in Susan's Volkswagen and headed for the armory at Norwich University. Now, as we stretched out and began running, we continued talking about the upcoming show season and what the goals were for the barn. We also talked about my job, which was something I could not avoid. It was Sunday, pretty much the only time off during the week I had at this point. The barn was closed on Sundays, which meant that the girls did not come up to ride or take care of the stalls. But after we ran, the two of us still had to do barn chores.

The armory at Norwich features an indoor track suspended over the well-polished floor below, which had three spaced, lined basketball courts where large groups could gather. It was also used for drill and was a ceremony area for the college. Although at each corner of the upstairs track was a door to exit in case of emergency, there was only one open that day and that was where everyone stepped onto the track. There were not that many students or others running, but it was only noon time, on a

Sunday. During the week, most students at Norwich began their day at 5 a.m. for PT (physical training).

Coming around the bend of the close turns, I noticed two men getting ready to step onto the track. It could get pretty tight, as it was merely a 1/10-mile span just four to five feet wide. As we came upon the two, it was a friendly gesture for me in such close quarters to raise my hand and form the words "hello."

His eyes were deep blue and piercing. His hair was dark brown. He was chiseled like a professional bodybuilder, lean and hard. His skin looked olive-toned. I got a sudden chill as he answered back "hi," and just as quickly, we ran past. Well, of course, he ran after me (we all had to go in the same direction). During the rest of the run, we engaged in casual conversation as the two men lapped past us or chose to lag behind making small conversation. Susan and I finished our run and headed down to the basement floor to the nautilus room of the same building. I was invigorated and a little giddy. *Gosh, he was so darn good looking.* There was something very physical about him that I liked. *Come on, Heidi, snap out of it, he was just running,* I thought, just as the two young men entered the room. I was drawn to speak to the dark-haired one first. He wasn't talking to some of the other very good-looking girls in the room; he was looking at and talking to me. "Would the two of you ladies like to go to the pub for a beer?" he asked. My immediate response, after feeling a patter of my heart beating all the way into my throat, was "we can't, we have stalls to clean." The disappointment did not show on his face as he turned to leave, probably thinking I was not at all interested, but then I said "but after we're done we would love to go." I hadn't even asked Susan, but she would go – *I would bribe her.* His face brightened up as he said "great." My hand reached out as he handed me a piece of paper with his name and phone number on it. His name was on the paper. In dark blue ink it was very nicely written, Jerry 485-4447. *What a nice name. He has much better handwriting than mine.*

I found myself zipping through the barn chores; thinking about the deep blue eyes, dark hair, and deep voice. Though he was wearing shorts and a shirt, I could see that his dark hairy arms had an olive hue to them. I finished my four stalls very quickly, took a shower, and looked at the clock. It was later than I thought. We had agreed on 3:00 p.m. and it was now 3:15. I called the number to the pub just to let Jerry know that we were running late. No answer. I dialed the pub number and left a message. *Good thing I lived in a small town.*

I hustled to the barn to get Susan, hopped into her Volkswagen, and headed down the hill into town.

We walked into the dimly lit Nantanna Pub. To the left were several cabaret tables and chairs. Also on the left was the bar, about twenty feet long. Beyond the bar were the bathrooms. To the right of the bathrooms there was one pool table, then the jukebox, a ten-by-ten dance floor, then another pool table, and tucked away near the exit were a couple more tables. There were hardly any people in the bar, but then again it was a Sunday afternoon. A couple of people, I knew. I waved "hi" to them and scanned the bar just in case I hadn't seen them, but saw no Jerry or his friend, whose name I did not know. Susan and I walked up to the bar. Julie, the owner, was standing opposite us and asked us what we wanted. We ordered a Michelob Light for me and a Corona for Susan. We sat over by the pool table in the cozy corner of the bar. *We are going to get stood up.* Just as I was thinking that, the two guys walked in. I waved and they walked over. They exchanged greetings and Susan said to Jerry's friend "I'm sorry I don't remember your name."

"Chris," he replied. Chris asked Jerry what he was having and walked up to the bar while Jerry pulled up a chair next to me.

"So, did you get all your barn chores done?" he asked.

"Yes," I replied. "We have students, who usually do the job, but on Sundays the barn is closed and someone has to clean up." Jerry seemed interested in finding out about the barn: How many horses? What kind? How long have I had them? Were just some of his questions.

"I had a bad experience with a horse once. I spent a day in the hospital after the horse I was riding ran me through a hallway. I hit my head on a beam and it knocked me out," Jerry said.

I learned his last name "DuChene" was French, but that he wasn't French. He was German and Irish. "I notice your name is Heidi Krause, is that German?" asked Jerry.

"Yes it is," I replied.

"My mother's maiden name was German. Her mom and dad are both German. We live in Ohio." Jerry stated.

"Oh, what part?"

"Dayton," he replied.

"Do you have any brothers or sisters?" I asked.

"Yes, I have four other siblings. I'm the oldest. I'm also the first one in my family to go to college and leave the state. My goal is to be a Marine."

"What makes you want to be a Marine?" I asked.

"My Uncle Ben lives in Missouri. He's retired now, but I have always wanted to be in the Marines. That's what made me want to come to a military school."

"Why not go to one of the academies, or VMI, or the Citadel?"

"Actually, I originally wanted to go to the Citadel, because my family goes to South Carolina every year in the summer. I came here because my old pediatrician is a professor at Dartmouth and he and my mother were talking about me and my interests. He mentioned Norwich to me and suggested I come up. My mother and I came out to visit. I liked it and well, here I am."

"What year are you?"

"I am a junior," Jerry replied.

"So what are your plans?" I asked.

"I go away to Parris Island, South Carolina this summer for boot camp. Then I'll be in the reserves next year. I want to be a boot, before I go as a commissioned officer," he explained.

"Why on earth would you do that?"

"Well, I would never want to ask someone to dig a trench for me if I couldn't get in and do it first."

"Hey, so how many kids do you want?" Jerry asked.

Yup, out of the blue, Jerry had managed to give me a line I had never heard before. His eyes danced as he asked it. *They looked through me. No... INTO me.*

"What?" I asked, astonished.

"I said, how many kids do you want to have? When we get married?" *Did I hear that right?*

I think I was probably as red as a boiled lobster, but Jerry was calm, cool, and collected. *Wow.* I was speechless.

It was as if Chris and Susan weren't even in the room. We just talked and listened, talked and listened. An hour went by quickly. Susan broke up the dreamy conversation by saying we should go: the horses needed to be fed. I just wanted to keep talking. He was so interesting.

I gave Jerry my phone number, written on the back of the Michelob Light label off the beer I had been drinking. I had peeled it off during the conversation.

"Is it possible for us to get a lift back to school? We walked down here. Neither one of us has a car," Jerry asked.

So that's why they were late, I thought. We had probably passed them.

Susan said, "Sure, hop in."

Bonus, I thought to myself. We could spend a few more minutes together.

We drove up the back of the small campus of Norwich to the "I beam" which was one of the gates to the upper parade ground and the military dorms. The dorms, made of brick, sat on a hill. Their main administrative building sat on the north side of the grounds, its face looking over the other buildings. It had a great big flag pole. To its left and right were dorms/barracks with names like Hawkins, Dodge, Patterson, Goodyear, Wilson, Alumni, and Gerard. They were named after various generals or contributors to the oldest private military college in the United States. I told Jerry how my own father had graduated from this college, founded by a former West Point graduate, and had gone on to earn his PhD in diplomatic history at Georgetown. Chris and Jerry got out of the car and thanked us for the ride.

"Can I call you, Heidi?" Jerry asked.

"I would like that." Wow did I sound funny. I watched as Chris and Jerry began their ascent up the incline to the dorms.

Susan exclaimed, "Well, that was fun, huh?" in her New Jersey sarcastic tone of voice.

"I told Chris that I'm getting married. It was nice talking with him. Did you have a nice conversation with Jerry?" I was on another planet, reliving our conversation and committing it to memory.

"Huh, ah, yes, it was very nice. I hope he calls me."

"Oh, I think he will. I heard him ask the how many kid thing. What a sweet talker. Now, just don't expect him to call you tonight, or tomorrow.... Maybe he'll call you in a week or so for a date next weekend."

We drove home the rest of the way in silence. I was a little weary from talking and a little lightheaded with my thoughts. Plus, I didn't really drink much alcohol because of my mother. Both of us finished the horses and I walked the fifty yards up the driveway to my father's dark home. I began my preparation for work the next day. I had to work with the cerebral palsy patient for 12 hours. My stomach began to ache as I thought about working and how fast this day had gone. The phone rang. It was Jerry.

"What are you doing?", he asked.

"Getting ready for work tomorrow, and you?"

"You know I thought you just worked with the horses. What do you do for work?"

"I'm a nurse. I work in people's homes taking care of sick children."

"Well, I was sitting here at my desk studying and I forgot whether or not I thanked you for a nice afternoon. I would like to go out with you again soon."

"I would like that. What are you doing this evening?" I could not believe I was saying this.

"Not a thing." Jerry said.

"Would you like to watch a movie?" I paused for a response. He said yes.

"Sure, can I come get you?"

"Yes, how about fifteen minutes? Meet at the I beam? Okay, great! See you soon." *Oh my God!!!! Can you believe how bold I was? I just met this guy. Oh well.*

So I got into my car and drove the three miles down the hill. The ruts from the day's mud had frozen a little. You still had to concentrate on the back roads, going slow, to avoid the mud sucking you into a rut and eating the car from the bottom up. I had heard about cars getting swallowed up in the mud season. It seemed like it took forever to get to the I beam. I half expected Jerry not to be there. But, as I pulled in I could see his five foot nine shadow walking down the same incline where I had watched him walk away only two hours before.

Jerry got in the car. "Hello," he said. He smelled nice, like he had just taken a shower and put on some aftershave.

"Did you get all your studying done?" I asked, sounding like such a mother. *Why do I do that?*

"Well, about as much as I could think and concentrate on. I'm a communications major; it's not that difficult."

"Oh, well, I hoped I wouldn't interrupt the studying," I said, as we went from pavement to dirt/mud.

Jerry seemed to grow quiet as I determinedly muckled on to the steering wheel a little tighter. We had also left behind the street lights of downtown and all you could see was darkness as the headlights of the car shone on the road. On the sides of the road there were lots of trees, but no houses, except every quarter mile or so. It's amazing that it didn't even occur to me that Jerry had no idea where I lived or where I was taking him. I pulled into the driveway, pointed to the barn, and said, "Well, that's where Susan lives. I live here." I pulled into the garage and turned off the engine. *Home sweet home.* "Come on in. I'll show you around."

"You live here by yourself?" Jerry asked.

"Yes, my father comes home once a month or so and I have a lot of people who check on me. Susan lives in the barn and there are two people who live in the back apartment on the other side of the house. We get along most of the time, but lately they're on my nerves. I have this protectiveness about my family and my father. My mom died in 1985 and I have more or less lived here by myself. Sometimes people have lived with me. My dad has some folks living here. They pay rent and for a few chores my Dad has reduced the rent by a hundred dollars. The only thing my dad expects is that the lawn gets mowed once a week. Jason only seems to mow when he feels like it. It seems to be he only mows when my father is coming up. It really bugs me, because it's hard on the mower when the grass is so long; then he has to rake it. If he just did it once a week he would be saving himself the work of raking, not to mention that a hundred dollars is a lot to get paid for mowing once a month. Listen to me carry on. I'm sorry."

"No, no, it's okay. I like hearing about you. I mow lawns back home. I actually do it for money. I'm more of a supervisor, though. I usually drop off my brothers Patrick or Philip and come back and collect the money. Out in Ohio it's a great way to earn some money. And you're right. It is hard on a mower. But see, if it's not his mower, it doesn't bother him."

"So, what movie do you want to see? I've got quite a selection. We only get three channels up here and no cable. My friend has taped a lot of different movies from HBO."

"It doesn't matter to me; I just want to get to know you better. Tell me more about you."

"Well, I work as a home care nurse for a professional nurses service. Right now I'm doing private duty nursing with pediatrics as a specialty."

"So, you graduated from where? Here at Norwich?"

"No, I went to the University of Vermont for four years. Then I moved to Rhode Island, where I worked at Rhode Island

Hospital in a "birth to two years of age" unit. I worked nights and it was too much for me. Nurses in big hospitals eat their young, so to speak. I got mono and ended up on leave for six weeks. I wanted to go back, but my doctor here insisted that if I go back I should go back to the days shift. You have to work a long time in a hospital of that size to have seniority enough to go straight days. They schedule for a rotation of either day/night or evening/night now. They would let me do adults days, but I really liked the floor I was on. So, I chose to come back here."

"Did you go to high school here in Northfield?"

"I've lived here since about the eighth grade. I know it's silly, but would you like to see some pictures? I have my yearbook."

"Sure. I didn't know they had a high school here, much less a yearbook."

"Well that's silly, why wouldn't we?"

"I guess it never really occurred to me that this is where people live, work, and go to school," Jerry said.

I rose from the couch where I had been sitting cross-legged and went downstairs to my room, where my photo albums were. I liked taking pictures and had several photo albums already. I grabbed a couple and headed back upstairs.

"Okay, I hope you're ready."

So, I began showing pictures of my life, as a little girl all the way up to high school and college. There is probably a dating law out there that says that this kind of date is illegal or something. The whole time Jerry never looked disinterested or bored. He sat and nodded, gave appropriate responses. I asked a couple of times if he wanted to stop and he said "No." We sat together on the couch, side by side. I never once felt uncomfortable. He balanced one side of the album on his knee and I had the other. From time to time our fingers would touch and that sent little electric currents shooting up my hands and arms. When we were almost finished with the yearbook, Jerry looked me in the eyes, commented how beautiful my blue eyes were, and leaned over and kissed me.

The next thing I knew I woke up, thinking I had just had the most awesome dream. I turned to my left to get out of bed and Jerry looked up at me from the floor (where he better have slept!) I thought to myself, "Wow!" I was in love and I think with my soul mate. I had to drop off Jerry at school for reveille. He was supposed to be at school when the bugler sounded out to account for his men. He held the rank of regimental command sergeant major in the corps of cadets, which meant in army terms he was the highest ranking NCO (non-commissioned officer) in the corps. The students in the corps of cadets held mandatory formation to take accountability every Monday morning. It was important for the cadet leaders to see who came back after the weekend. There was only one regimental command sergeant major and that was Jerry.

I am not proud of the fact that I have had a couple of one-night stands in the past, which left me feeling awful the next morning, not to mention ashamed, embarrassed, and disgusted with myself. This was not one of those feelings. I was absolutely invigorated. Jerry and I were talking, not just small talk. He was interested in my life; interested in who I was, not just getting in the sack with someone. It was as if we had been together for a very long time. He kissed me when I dropped him off and he left asking me if he could call me again later. I said a quick astonished yes, as I really wanted him to call or else I would be devastated. I headed off to what promised to be a very long shift, after staying up so late.

The whole commute was filled with thoughts about the night before. I replayed everything dozens of times in my head. When I got to my patient's home my patient's mother noticed my "spark" and commented on how happy I looked. I worked only six hours and headed home. My eight hours included my travel on this day. Then all the way home I thought about Jerry and wondered in anticipation if he would call.

When I got home, the light was blinking on my answering machine. I had three messages. One from Susan wondering why I hadn't called the night before, one hang up, and one from my father. *Bummer, Jerry didn't call.* As I changed my clothes and wondered if I should go running, the phone rang.

"Hi. It's Jerry. How was your day?"

Oh my! Was I relieved!

For the next two weeks we spent quite a bit of time together. When I wasn't working I was with him. Jerry would go to class and then I would either pick him up or he would get a ride. He was leaving for home for almost two weeks of spring break. He asked me to take him to the airport and I said I would. *Gosh I was going to miss him.*

It was the night before he was leaving and he came up and we made dinner together. Most of Jerry's friends were at the bar and he had let his friends down by coming up to spend time with me. His friends had made reference to him "shacking up" with some girl, but it did not seem to bother him except that he was mentioning it, which kind of bothered me.

"I'm going to miss you, Heidi," he said as he kissed me and hugged me.

I knew I loved him, but everything was moving fast and he was leaving. I was going to have to set myself up for letdown. I just kissed him back and said, "I'll miss you too," even though I was just jumping up and down inside. I couldn't help but think about what some of his friends had said about me. One of them had told me about Jerry's reputation with the ladies at Norwich. "He is promiscuous and non-committing: a ladies man." I didn't want to believe that he was leading me on, just to have a good time, but I had this intense gut feeling that he was the one I would marry.

I had had a couple of serious boyfriends in high school and college. In high school, I went out with a guy one year older than I was and he went off to join the navy. We were together for four years. His name was Kevin and when he left for the navy, he gave me the "you should date other people" speech. Yet, whenever he came home, I would see him. I also went with his mother to see him graduate at the Great Lakes navy basic training. During this time, I had dated other people on and off. One in particular also went to Norwich.

His name was Clark and he was from Rhode Island. He was a very nice man, unless he was drinking. When he had been drinking he turned into a real jerk. He became obnoxious, verbal, and dominant. When I moved to Providence, Rhode Island to work, he was living there. He had a house with two other guys. I would work nights and would see him occasionally on my days off. I also would see him on some evenings. A part of me knew about the odds of either becoming an enabler to an alcoholic or becoming alcoholic myself, but there was also a part of him I was very attracted to. On one particular evening, the census was slow on my floor, so it was my turn to be called off my shift. So, I got in my car and drove out towards his house, near Newport. I pulled in and saw someone's car I did not recognize, but figured it was one of the other roommates. I walked up to the front door and before I knocked I couldn't help but peer in the side window next to the door. There was Clark in a very compromising position on top of some woman. I drove back to my apartment in Providence in tears and pretty much never spoke to Clark again. I never did tell him why. I had told him that I loved him. He had never told me how he felt. I just didn't know any better. So back to Kevin, my high school sweetheart, I went; the one everyone in my hometown said I would be together with forever. It was more long distance, but we seemed closer than ever. His sister and I would often talk about marriage proposals. It was during this long-distance and short-visit romance that I met Jerry. Now, he was too good to be true!

Cautiously, I did not respond with my gut feeling by wrapping myself up with Jerry and telling him I thought he was a wonderful man. And I was going to marry him. That is, if he felt the same way after spring break.

So, I drove Jerry and one of his friends to the airport. It was a quiet ride. *I really did not like separation.* I always had this little anxiety. Yet every time someone in my life came or went, this would happen. I dropped him off, giving him a really nice kiss and hug. It was a tender, yet passionate kiss; but not dramatic or anything one would expect to see in a movie. I could feel the intensity of it and driving away in tears, longed to be kissed like that soon. That kiss would have to hold me over until Jerry got back. So, I drove away, thought about the last couple of weeks, and listened to the radio. While I was driving, a song by Bryan

Adams came on the radio. I began listening to the words of the song

"Look into your heart, you will find

There's nothing there to hide." Could I be falling this hard? This song is getting to me I'm thinking how this guy seems to look inside my soul. The song kept going and as it did I listened to the words to the song, I started seeing flashes of my future. At least a dream future. I saw me walking down the aisle with Jerry in his Marine Corps uniform. I saw swords. I saw men doing hand-to-hand combat. I saw me having a baby with Jerry at my side. (Wow. I had quite an imagination.)

I had that vision every time I heard that song. I've had it ever since.

The two weeks went by quickly. I hadn't heard from him and it was getting close to him coming home. I couldn't remember if he had asked me to pick him up, so making a bold move, I called him at home in Ohio.

"Hello, my name is Heidi Krause. I was wondering if I could speak with Jerry.... Yes, thank you." *(She mentioned that Jerry had mentioned me. Was that good or bad, I thought.)*

"Heidi? Hi. How is everything? Gosh, I forgot to ask you if you would pick me up. I can't believe I forgot. Would you please? I come in on USAir to Burlington on Sunday. Yes, a four o'clock flight. I would really appreciate it. I can't wait to see you. See you in a couple of days." Then we said goodbye and we hung up. I was happy to have spoken to him; hearing his voice was just wonderful. Yet, there was no mention of love or marriage.

The next two days could not have been any slower. All I thought about was Jerry and I could hardly concentrate. Susan kept me in reality by having me help with the horses and I also kept busy at the gym. Sunday afternoon came along and I drove the hour it usually takes to get to Burlington International Airport. I parked the car in the lot and decided to walk casually around the airport. There were several Norwich men I could see arriving. *I wondered how they all got back.* Just as I was thinking that, I spotted Jerry at the luggage area, talking with his friend Paul. Paul was in the navy and had spent two weeks in training on a submarine. After a quick kiss and some hugs, Jerry re-introduced me to him. Then he asked if I would mind giving him a ride back to campus. So, the ride back was filled with Paul and Jerry talking about their vacations and me just listening. It was okay though, because I was with the man I loved.

The ride went faster with all the talking and I pulled into Norwich just as it was getting dark. Paul apparently lived in the same dorm/barracks as Jerry. Jerry invited me to his room; apparently he had his own. It was pretty nice, for a military-style room. His room had a bunk bed in it. One bunk was spotless and was made precisely as required by the school. You could bounce a quarter off the mattress. The bed had a white pillow at the head and the wool maroon and gold blanket with "Norwich" right in the center of it. It was usual for the "Norwich" to center at the chest portion on the bed. He informed me that this particular bed saved him time, especially for room inspections which were done every Tuesday morning. The other bed had sheets on it, but on top of it was a grey sleeping bag. Jerry said that was usually where he slept (when he didn't stay over at my house). Jerry excused himself for a minute and I glanced further around his room. Pictures of his family were under his desk blotter. A picture of a Marine also was on it. My number was also under the blotter. I noticed an ash tray with some butts in it. A pack of Camels was near the ash tray. In the short time I had known Jerry, I had not seen him smoke, nor had I smelled it on his clothes or on his breath. I am usually very good at detecting smoke. My mother had smoked and I detested it. I decided I was going to say something to him, when he walked back into the room. We talked a little small talk, and I guess my look gave me away.

"What's wrong?"

"I didn't know you smoked?" I said.

"Well, I do when I need to be up all night," he explained.

"Jerry, I really hate that. I respect that you're honest, but I have seen the worst of what smoking can do to you, even on occasion. I mean eww! I used to hate it when my mother smoked. The smell is still in the curtains at the house." I was shocked that Jerry even smoked. Jerry was a handsome, olive-skinned, blue-eyed muscle machine. I referred to him as GQ gorgeous. I used to catch him on the porch looking at his reflection in the big picture window which looked out on the beautiful mountains of Vermont. He looked at the reflection of his body, while making a muscle. He couldn't see in the window, but I sure could see out!

"I'm sorry. My father smoked for a long time, while he was in his band and the Air Force. My Grandpa Duchene also smoked pretty heavy – also Camels. He died a few years ago. He also had diabetes and drank quite a bit. I think what killed him was the fact that he was so active that when he had to have his legs amputated, it killed him."

I never saw Jerry smoke again. Thank God.

Later that evening, Jerry came up to my house. He was reflective, intense, and did not say much. I let him be, just holding on to him, kissing him gently on the cheek from time to time. After about an hour of cuddling, I noticed Jerry begin to sweat, and since my head was on his bare chest his heart rate increase. He rolled over on top of me and with tears in his eyes, said "Heidi, I have been waiting to tell you from the moment I met you that I love you. I want to marry you. Will you marry me?"

Well, not quite what I had expected to come out of Jerry's mouth. I was left speechless.

All I could say was "We haven't known each other that long. Ask me again tomorrow, when you have had a chance to sleep on it." *I was just dumbfounded. Did he have too much to drink?* How did I say such a stupid thing? Of course I wanted to marry this man. He was my soul mate. I just knew it. Had I just broken his heart? What loser had ever said "ask me again in the morning"? I had trouble sleeping the whole night. I was reeling with emotion and just wanted to wake Jerry up and tell him how silly I was to have said what I did. 5 a.m. arrived and the alarm went off. Jerry needed to be down at school and I needed to make the 90-mile journey to Island Pond today. Jerry didn't say much as he jumped into the shower. I went upstairs to make the coffee and let the dogs out. As I poured two cups of the coffee for us, I suddenly felt a sensation of warmth, a presence behind me. It was Jerry. *Boy, was he stealthy.* "Well, it is morning, and I couldn't sleep a wink last night. Heidi, I love you. Will you marry me? I don't have a ring, and don't know when I can afford to get one. When I was in Ohio, I could think of nothing more than you and spending the rest of my life with you. What do you say?"

"Jerry, from the moment you asked me out, I connected with you and said to myself, this is the man I will marry. I am just overwhelmed by how lucky I am to have found you. Yes, I will marry you."

We shared a hug and a very passionate kiss. I finished my coffee, got ready to leave, and took Jerry down to school. Then I made my long journey to Island Pond. I was on cloud nine the whole day, dreaming of my wedding, thinking about how beautiful it would be. Of course, there was much to do. Jerry still needed to finish college and then be a Marine. Of course I would follow him; as a nurse I could get a job anywhere. The song from Bryan Adams came on again as I drove to Island Pond.

That night Jerry called his parents from the house and told them. They sounded excited, a little different than I expected. They sounded so very nice on the phone. I talked with Jerry's Mom and Dad, Emily, Patrick, Philip, and Laura – who Jerry called Lolly. We discussed dates and places and ideas, but set nothing in stone.

My father was another story. I called my sister and told her, but my Dad wanted an old-fashioned "ask for his daughter's hand in marriage" talk. He wanted to learn more about this Jerry person I was so in love with. He was scheduled to come up to Vermont soon and Jerry and he would get to know one another. They would walk "the hill." The hill was a draw of a mountain where we lived and where we had the horses. It was about 133 acres of heaven in the mountains of Vermont. You could see for miles on clear days. Jerry wanted to spend some time with my father first, getting to know him, and then on another visit he would take "that walk." The next day my father was scheduled to come into the airport. Being the middle of the week, I agreed to go and get him. He would usually come do chores. Over the weekend we could relax and talk a little.

Jerry and my father had actually met briefly before "the talk." I was so nervous for him. My dad was tough. I remember he rarely had to discipline me as a teen because he had toughness about him. He had been through war, he was an intellectual, he was hard to approach as a parent, because I saw him as a respectful, sort of perfect guy, who never ever made mistakes, and what he said you did not question. He also had very thick eyebrows. As I got older, all I had to do was see the brow on his right eye go up and I was stopped in my tracks. Of course there was no warning Jerry. His mind was set.

They briefly shook hands. My dad had a box in his hand and two sets of clippers, which he had set down to shake Jerry's hand. My dad suggested Jerry pick the box up and assist him and also suggested that while they walked they would work on one of the trails to the middle apple orchard pasture where he would later turn out the horses to graze. It was nothing for him to trek several times up the hill with the horses, which was a good two hundred yards from our house! He was in great shape for a man of forty-nine. He often ran thirteen miles a day and had run several marathons.

A few hours later they came down. *Relief, Jerry was alive*! My dad announced to me that he gave Jerry his blessing and gave me a kiss on the cheek. We all shared dinner and Jerry called his parents. Dad and Jerry now had a funny "bonding" story to tell. Apparently as Jerry was walking up the mountain, he was being grilled by my father about Jerry's intentions with me. As he was walking, he would occasionally feel a jolt coming from the box. Jerry thought it was his nerves, but every minute or so the jolt got more intense as the now "charged" solar battery electric fence charger for the upper pasture was turned on and began to give him jolts of electricity. Finally Jerry, stopped, exclaimed "Sir! What is this thing?" and set the solar powered unit down. My dad sauntered over to the contraption and exclaimed "Oh, my apologies, the 'on' button was in the on position!" They had formed a bond that day and enjoyed the laugh together while sitting over dinner. I would take Jerry to the airport in the morning and then he was off to Parris Island, South Carolina for thirteen weeks of training. He would essentially be out of contact with his family and me for that time. He would be able to write, but not often, and calling was a reward he would earn over several weeks. That night Jerry was ill. He vomited, had diarrhea; "all nerves," he said. I still did not understand why people would put themselves through this grueling test of mental strength and physical strain and drain all to become a Marine. Jerry actually did not have to go to Parris Island. Because he was in college, he could have applied to the Basic School (TBS), like some of his other classmates. Not Jerry though. He had it in his head that to be a good leader he would endure everything from the bottom up.

The next day Jerry left from Burlington. *Thirteen weeks and counting*, I thought.

The first couple of weeks went by. I worked and hung out with the horses and in the barn in my free time. I also began planning the wedding of my dreams. I went to dress shops and even bought two dresses that I really believed were going to be my bridesmaids'. They were mostly navy blue dresses with mauve flowers and puffy shoulders. One dress was just Laura's size, so I bought it instantly, because after all Laura would be in the wedding and this shop was going out of business.

I talked a few times with Jerry's mother on the phone, when she called to chat and to get to know me. I told her all about the dress and plans that I was making.

"Do you have a date?" She would ask. *I hadn't really thought of a date, but knew I had always liked spring and summer weddings. I really wished my mom was around to help in planning.* Another thing I was doing was attending adult catechism classes. I had been in the process of converting from Protestant to Catholic. It was a decision that I had started to make while at college. Once a week I would go to the chapel on campus and take classes with several others with a priest, Father Lavalley, who was one of the chaplains at Norwich.

One of the reasons he said he became a priest was because of my adopted grandfather, who had been a Philosophy Religion and Fine Arts professor at Norwich and was the chaplain at Norwich for a long time before he died. Father Lavalley is probably the one driving-force type of individual that I know who is considered an evangelical catholic. I used to ask him why we had to memorize all the prayers and he told me to "pray what is in your heart." So I did.

At the end of the summer (thirteen weeks – I had never really thought much about how many weeks were in the summer before), Jerry's mother called and invited me to meet them and stay with them first in South Carolina when Jerry graduated and then in Ohio to meet the rest of the family. I would be with them for the remainder of the summer until Jerry needed to report back to Norwich. That was almost two weeks. I eagerly said yes. My father interjected, saying "fish stinks after three days."

I hadn't a clue what he was talking about and asked him to explain. "You should go, meet his family, and stay only a couple of days. You don't want to wear out your welcome," he said.

I did not listen to him. I excitedly went to Parris Island, South Carolina to meet and greet my in-laws to be. They met me at the airport. I met Jerry's mom whose name is Sharon and dad (Jerry Sr.), Emily, Philip, and Laura. Patrick had stayed back in Ohio to work (the landscape business was in full swing) and he played soccer, so he needed to stay for practices.

Jerry's mother is very pretty, I thought. Her features were kind, grayish blue eyes, short hair, and slender build. She also had the legs of a dancer. While getting to know Jerry I had learned that Jerry's mom was a dancer. She had worked in a dance school and went to beauty pageants. I learned later she shared the very same birthday as my mother (March 1).

Jerry's father was the spitting image of an older version of Jerry. He was named for him. Jerry was the Jr. How striking he looked. He was the same height with muscular build, blue eyes, and graying hair. I had also learned that Jerry's father was in a four-member band called "The Four Saints." He played the trumpet and sang. He had met Jerry's mother while touring in Ohio. He had been married before and lost his first wife to Leukemia. When he had first met Jerry's mother, she was eighteen and dating a man named Jack from the University of Dayton.

Emily was the spitting image of her mother. She was tall, slender, tan and had soft features. I remember Jerry telling me it was his wish that his sister became a nun. She was the "good" child of the family in Jerry's eyes and in his opinion, could do no wrong. Jerry really loved his sister. He was also very protective of her. When some of the other students at Norwich asked about his sister coming for a ball, he got in their faces and kindly told them that his sister was not for any cadet, she was going to be a nun.

Philip, the youngest brother, stood about four foot, nine inches tall, golden brown tan with brown hair and had those same piercing blue eyes Jerry did, as well as the eyebrows. You could tell that Philip really looked up to his brother. Currently, he had his hair cut in a "high and tight" style, as the Marines did.

Laura had opaque colored skin, with freckles and red hair cut in a short bob. She stood about four feet tall. Jerry called her "Lolly" and you could tell how much Jerry loved his Lolly. Laura was born with Down syndrome and had had heart surgery when Jerry was a freshman at Norwich.

They met me at the airport and I was very glad to meet them. We went to eat and freshen up and then we were able to see Jerry for a short time for a "liberty." He could not leave the base, but would show us all the places he had spent time in the short thirteen weeks he was there. I don't remember much of the dinner, but we went into the visitors' center, and waited for the short list of names to be called. We were called in to a room and Jerry came in. He was wearing his tan pants and a shirt and tie. It was sooo good to see him. I know we shared the same relief that the summer was over. Jerry kissed his mother, his father, Lolly, Emily, and Philip and all the while he had his eyes on me. I noticed Jerry's mom look over at me. I noticed the look she had on her face while Jerry glanced at me. I'm sure it was a test. He came over to me, hugged me tightly, and kissed me right on the lips in front of them all. Later, I learned that Jerry had not done that to anyone before, so the whole family was a little shocked. While on this liberty, Jerry showed us the PX (Post Exchange), the tarmac, where he would graduate the next day, the cafeteria, where he ate, and his barracks. He introduced us to his drill sergeants and other staff. I'm ashamed to say that I don't have a clue what their names were. I was just taking it all in. It was from the drill sergeants that we all learned that Jerry had broken Parris Island records for pull-ups and pushups. I did say before that he was really well-built.

Before Jerry had gotten the rank of command sergeant major at Norwich, he worked out hard. He looked chiseled, perfectly chiseled. His absolute hero was the cadet colonel, named Michael. Michael was a very intimidating young man, whose voice was commanding, and he was stacked. Every muscle showed in great definition. Even at twenty-two, he had no hair. Jerry had admitted to me that the two of them had done "a cycle or two of steroids." It was to look the part for the corps. For that position, according to the two of them, you had to be hard. Look hard and be hard.

Jerry's figure had gotten even more chiseled then before he left. I don't think there was one fat deposit left, not that there was much before.

We left that evening, scheduled to be back in the morning. We all went back to the hotel. Emily and I shared a room with two double beds and Laura, Philip, and Mr. and Mrs. Duchene shared the other. I remember Emily being so careful not to let her feet touch the floor, citing that her mother had informed her of all the diseases you could catch in hotels. I hadn't really thought much about it. My family and I didn't stay in hotels, we camped. I remember Jerry telling me that his mother's idea of camping was sitting in the lobby of a hotel with all the plants around. I recall being asleep and having a dream that a phone had rung, someone had died. I sat up in bed, and asked Emily who had died. She told me I was dreaming. It must have been the TV show she was watching and I went back to sleep.

In the morning, Jerry's mother came to our room and told Emily that Jerry's grandmother had passed away the night before and the funeral would be in Missouri in a few days. Emily gave me a look I will never forget. She was obviously weirded out that I somehow knew. She mentioned it to her mother. *Oh well, I'm a freak. What can I say?* I told Jerry's mother that I would travel back home and she insisted that I should come with them. "You will get a chance to meet the rest of the family." I dropped the issue.

Graduation was hot, especially on the bleachers on the black tarmac. One of Jerry's friends, Todd from Norwich had also attended. They hadn't really been very close, but it appeared that the Parris Island experience had bonded them just like rook buddies were at Norwich (freshman incoming students going into the corps of cadets are referred to as "rooks"). This was camaraderie with which no one except other rook buddies could associate. Jerry and Todd would be in the same reserve unit back in Manchester, New Hampshire when they went back to school.

After packing all of us into their Buick station wagon, we made the long journey back to Dayton, Ohio. When we got to Dayton, I stayed with Nanny and Bampa, Jerry's grandparents (Jerry's mother's parents). Jerry absolutely adored and worshipped the ground his Nanny and Bampa walked on.

Nanny was a lot shorter than Jerry had recounted. She stood about four feet nine inches tall and in her age she had started to hunch forward. Her gray hair was up on her head in a perfect bun every time I saw her; a very typical German descendent. She was proper and adored Jerry as much he did her. Jerry was the oldest of five of her daughter's children and had spent a lot of time with Nanny and Bampa, as his father would be on tour and his mother traveled with the band. Jerry Jr. even had a tuxedo for himself, when he was four or five.

Bampa was a stoic man, very quiet, but one of the kindest men I have ever met. He was so very much like my adopted grandfather. You could see the love and adoration he had for Jerry. I hadn't mentioned it before, but Jerry was very glad to speak of his Bampa, how it was his truck they used for mowing, how his grandfather was a builder and had built many of the buildings around Dayton and surrounding areas. He had also built the house. I was going to stay in Jerry's mother's old room. The whole house was so neat. The living room carpet had the largest and thickest carpet pile I have ever seen. You could write your name in the carpet and it would stay there. There was lots of finished wood on the walls and a den to the right as you entered. Nanny liked to listen to the baseball games on the radio and watch them on TV. Jerry had told me about a boxer dog Nanny and Bampa had when he was younger, named "Captain." He used to say that the dog was so strong that he would lift up the garage door. The dog was deceased now, but there were pictures of him and the dog on the TV.

The room I was staying in had paneling on the walls and lots of stuffed animals on the bed. There was another bedroom that was for Bruce, Jerry's uncle, who now lived in Florida with his wife and two children.

The bathroom I was using was the cleanest I have ever experienced. I was almost afraid to use it. The morning after we arrived in Dayton, Jerry came over in the morning to pick me up. Instead of going to the front door, he strode over to the back and peeked in the kitchen window. I heard Nanny squeal with enjoyment, as it was reminiscent of the old days when Jerry would do that when he came over, as Nanny was frequently in the kitchen. He walked in, kissed Nanny, and went to the fridge, where, when he swung open the door, there were 8 oz. coca cola bottles. They were cold and tasted "the best." Nanny told Jerry he couldn't have one so early, in a teasing fashion, and Jerry grabbed one, popped it open, and took a swig. With a big smile on his face, he asked Nanny if she would join us for breakfast at Denny's. We were going to spend a day in Dayton and then tomorrow head for the funeral. All of us, in the Buick station wagon. There would be eight of us, because Patrick was going too.

Nanny declined and Jerry and I headed for Denny's, where we met Jerry's mother, Emily, and Laura. After eating, we separated and Jerry took me on a tour of Dayton, including the house Jerry lived in before heading to school. We drove by it. It had just sold, apparently, and Jerry's family had moved into a townhouse near Nanny's house. The houses in Dayton were very nice. In Oakwood, Jerry showed me all the expensive mansion homes and the school that Emily and he had attended. Jerry had a key to the Oakwood home. We walked around the brick walkway he and his dad had made and he told me that his Bampa had built the home. They had sold the house, because as Jerry explained his mom and dad had gone bankrupt, between the managers of The Four Saints keeping two books and having to sell the hotel they owned in Miami where they stayed and played, plus paying for Laura's surgery (she had to have open-heart surgery related to her Down syndrome). Jerry really loved this house. He hated telling me that they had to move. He didn't want me to think ill of his parents. *I didn't at all*. He kissed me and said, "Maybe someday you and I could live in this house." I thought, if Jerry's parents couldn't afford to live in Oakwood, then we certainly couldn't at this point in our lives. But it was a nice dream and Jerry was so tender with his thoughts. They were familial thoughts.

We started out the next day for Missouri. I think in retrospect this was not a good trip to have made with my future in-laws. *My father was right*. I really enjoyed meeting Jerry's Uncle Ben, Aunt Florene, and their families. I don't remember much about the funeral or the trip, except the car was packed. The journey from Ohio to Missouri was flat, barren, and hot. The reception was in a BBQ restaurant. Uncle Ben and Aunt Florene seemed to live in the only hilly area of Missouri. There was a lake and going up and down winding hilly roads, Jerry's mom and Emily (Emily seemed to mirror or mimic everything her mother did) seemed judgmental about things. It was like they were on their best behavior before, but took on a whole new life. I tried to not say anything; I tried to fit in. Uncle Ben and Aunt Florene were decent, solid, "tell it like it is" people. They have children who are in dysfunctional families and have disabilities, but they love them and show them off to others. Jerry's family in comparison seemed like a very proud family. They were different here than in Dayton. It seemed they had to act perfectly and as I observed, it was evident to me that Jerry's mom had a very tight hold on everything the family did or said. In conversations, nothing was ever shared about imperfections, even the loss of the house.

As soon as we got back to Ohio, I definitely felt a change of attitude on Jerry's mom's part towards me. She was pleasant, but was short with me. After we returned I was dropped off at Nanny's and Bampa's and Jerry would come over and get me, spend the day, eat and return to his parents.

On one of the days we went into Dayton to a water park. Jerry and I rented a canoe, and Jerry paddled around the park. We were alone.

"Jerry, I've noticed since we got back from Missouri that your family hasn't been that warm to me. Did I do something wrong?" I said.

"No, it's not *you,* but it is. The way I see it is that my mom and you are way too much alike, yet she sees that I will be leaving, getting married and it will be with you."

I kept my silence thinking to myself, *I'm not trying to be clinical here, but Jerry I think your mother doesn't just love you, she is in love with you.* I knew that I really shouldn't have made that kind of judgment and felt bad. I didn't want to hurt him even more because I could see this was bothering him.

"That is part of the problem. My mom and dad and brothers and sisters had a family meeting. They sat around after we got back and basically came at me with the fact they don't like you, they think you're not right for me, you act differently around them than you do with just me. They think you're too clinical around Laura, you did this weird thing down at Parris Island that my sister thinks you're some witch. Basically they told me they don't want anything to do with you and for the rest of your stay I'm not to bring you around the house. They want me to break off the engagement with you.... I'm beside myself. I have never gone against them before. They are my family. I don't know what to do." He continued to paddle the canoe; small amounts of sweat on his chest and the sunlight made him kind of sparkle.

Wow, I wasn't liked. My dad had been right about not going longer than a few days … remembering his exact quote. "Fish stinks after three days!!!!"

"Well what are you going to do?" I asked with tears in my eyes.

"Honeyness, I am as shocked as you are," he said in a soft broken-hearted voice.

Jerry had developed this nickname before leaving for Pariss Island. He often wrote to me and called me his darling "Honeyness." I am still not entirely sure why.

I was silent, dumfounded. It seemed as though they liked me, especially Jerry's Uncle Ben and Aunt Florene. If we did get married, I wondered how I could handle rejection.

"Well, if that is what you want, then we will break up. I thought I was being myself. I'm sorry if they feel I am too clinical," I said.

"I'm going to enjoy the remainder of your stay here. I grew up here. I want to show you all about my life here. You are the one person I want to share my life with; **both** my lives. You know me in Vermont and I want to show you who I am here. Can you do that? "

Jerry said this with much drama in his hands and facial expression. His eyes were looking deep into my soul when he asked that question.

I sat there watching him paddle the canoe, his olive-tone, tan, muscled arms scraping the water, first piercing the surface, pulling his biceps backward, causing the boat to propel forward. Then he would take the paddle up out of the water and do the same thing on the opposite side. This kept us going in a pretty even straight line down "the river."

I watched him do this for several strokes before I answered. "Yes, I can, but I just want to tell you that we are in for a long road."

"I think I can handle it. I'm a Marine." Jerry said.

So, that is what we did for the rest of my stay. That night Jerry wanted to go hear an old fashioned big band playing in Kettering, called Lincoln Park. The band was going to play music from the big band era. This park area had assisted living and nursing homes, as well as condos. There was a nice park and a pond area. Many activities happened at this park. One of the things Jerry wanted to do was to see and listen to and dance to a band similar to his father's band. Jerry dressed in his Marine Corps khaki uniform and I wore a sun dress. We danced the night away, as many older women and men did. Jerry looked so handsome in his uniform. We were the youngest couple there and it was only a little uncomfortable soaking in the stares from older couples, but maybe they were thinking of themselves at a younger age.

I went home and started my usual back to work routine, as I wondered if things would be different. Jerry would be coming back to Vermont within a week to start cadre week for his senior year. Two of his best friends in the corps, Les and Art, were the big leaders at the school, having been promoted in the spring before school got out. The two of them were also Marines, but when they graduated they would receive commissions as officers. Jerry was going to be the provisional battalion executive officer, in charge of the public relations part of the corps. It was not as involved as his previous position, but Les and Art felt that Jerry could spend more time with me and concentrate on being in the Marine Corps Reserve.

When Jerry arrived back to Vermont, even though I picked him up at the airport, he seemed different.

"So, what's wrong?" I asked.

"Nothing; I'm sure glad to be back," he answered.

We didn't say much to each other on the forty-five minute trek back to Northfield. I dropped Jerry off at his dorm. He kissed me and told me he would call me later, when he had done all his paperwork, made his bed, and got all of his things in order. I left in tears, not knowing if we had broken up, or what. Rather than going off the deep end, I decided just to go home and get ready for the work week. Honestly, I did not know if I would ever hear from Jerry again.

Several hours later, as I sat in the bottom floor room of my parent's house I watched the one channel of television that we got in the basement. The room I lived in faced the front, part of the original house in which my grandfather had lived. We had built an addition to the back of it. It had a window facing west, with a great view of Scragg Mountain. It also had a bathroom with shower. Although I had grown up in the back part of the house, sharing a bathroom with my sister, I felt uncomfortable out back because I could not hear if cars came in to the driveway as quickly as in the front. Besides, my dad had rented the downstairs apartment and it was accessible from the library's spiral staircase opening in front of my sister's room. I had felt like I was constantly eavesdropping on the tenants. So I moved to the basement of the main part of the house. A good thing about the basement was that it was cooler in the summer and felt cozy in the winter. I had a bathroom with a shower, closet, and nice picture window facing west, where the driveway came in from the main road.

The program wasn't anything interesting and I was just in a grumpy, foul, confused mood. I had never felt sort of heartbroken like this before, not knowing if I even was. How confused am I? Anyway, headlights hit the back of the wall and I heard a car pull in, some voices, and someone got out and said thanks. Then I heard the sound of the mud room door.

In the east, we have mud rooms. A "mud room" is a room that you can enter during all the different seasons: Winter, Mud season, Spring, Summer, Fall. It is essential for folks in the country on the many back roads of Vermont, since they are mostly dirt. It also helps keep heat in so you can take your coats shoes, etc. off. Farmers are very smart and by taking off their outer farm layer – especially their shoes, which had walked around in God knows what throughout the day – and leaving it in the mud room, they can keep mud out of the house. I once swept the concrete floor of my dad's garage and got a metal waste can full of dirt that I had to dump back onto the driveway. Most of Vermont has mud rooms, unless you have a farmhouse with a dirt floor, or you're a "flatlander," and then you just clean all the time.

I heard steps coming from upstairs traveling across the slate kitchen floor and then the living room, opening the sliding pocket door of the stairwell, and then down each step. My heart was beating fast and I had this fluttery feeling in my stomach. I looked up from my bed and it was Jerry. "Hi Honeyness!" he said.

He walked closer and I stood up and melted into his tall frame (I am only five foot three inches tall). He kissed me tenderly on the mouth.

"I really missed you," he said, as he took his right hand, held the left side of my face, and looked me in the eyes *right into my soul again* with his own dark blue ones.

"I didn't think I would hear from you tonight, if ever. I felt so awful when I dropped you off."

"I had a lot on my mind and I just needed to get some things out of my head," Jerry answered.

"Anything you care to talk about?" I asked. On one perspective I was interested in knowing, but on the other, I didn't want my heart to get broken. Yet, he had just kissed me so passionately that if Jerry stayed it was going to be very hard to have him sleep next to me in the trundle bed without going any further before we were married. *That is, if we still are getting married*, I thought.

"Not really, but I did talk with Art and Les. I'm working on it. I will let you know." He answered.

"Did I do something, or does it have to do with me anyway?" I said. *It has to be something involving his family, or me.*

Jerry got this really pitiful look on his face (a face not many people got to see), like he was just so concerned, and said "Honeyness, no. You haven't done anything. I'll let you know."

I couldn't help but feel better, but I still knew it had something to do with me. Jerry had had the look I think I had when I was in ROTC in college and was down in boot camp knowing I was supposed to be fulfilling someone else's wishes, but being miserable and distant, knowing that it was really your life and not being ready to make a choice and disappoint your parents.

I was the elder of two girls. My father and stepmother had told me if I got an ROTC scholarship, they would get me a car. I remember being thrilled with the idea of having my own car. I looked and looked at cars. I was in love with a Volkswagen Cabriolet convertible. My grades were good, but I didn't qualify my first year at UVM. I took all the ROTC classes and physical training and eventually got a three-year scholarship. Instead of that brand new car, my parents gave me the blue Subaru hatchback that I was already able to use. I was miserable. To take ROTC meant I was carrying military classes and not getting credits toward my Nursing degree. So, not only was I taking more classes, but I was also waking up every morning for either nursing clinical or PT. My dad used to teach us that once we made a commitment, we should make the most of it and follow it through. So, I continued. We were on a combined field training exercise one spring before the end of my junior year. I was due to go to advanced camp, to the Nurses Battalion part, which was six weeks at Fayetteville, North Carolina. The training first took place at Fort Bragg and then moved on to clinical internships. My clinical was going to be at Walter Reed Medical Center. The Green Mountain Battalion of UVM was in a combined exercise with Norwich University and Dartmouth. The squad I was in was doing some orienteering called "land navigation," when I twisted my ankle. Both of my ankles had been injured in high school playing soccer. My ankle was not swollen or bruised very badly, but just to be on the safe side the Battalion Commander, our PMS (professor of military science), told me to sit out in the Quonset hut during the night-time land navigation piece.

There was an army drill staff sergeant (Sergeant Mooney), a Special Forces chap from Norwich who kept me busy by having me take apart my M16 and put it back together. His goal for me was to do this in under a minute and then he was going to have me try it blindfolded. It was during this time that he mentioned to me that nurses don't have to do all THIS STUFF. Nope, no lying around in ditches, in the mud, while snow was falling on you in the spring, waiting for an ambush or land navigation, or anything IF I went into the service as a direct commission instead of ROTC; "all the nurses and doctors can do that," he said. *Now they tell me*. I decided that I shouldn't have done any of this. I wasn't really cut out for this kind of thing. I knew I was committed and was going to make the best of it, but if I had been given a choice, I probably would have gone for the other route, or none of this. There were two really good things for which I was thankful. One, I had met many really nice people and two, I learned how to rappel. As I am afraid of heights, this was an outstanding test of trust of self and others.

I went down to Fayetteville, North Carolina, where it was sooo hot and humid; it was like wearing a wet paper towel night and day around your body. You could never get dry. Within the first couple of days after arrival each company of nurses went to the hospital for an eight-hour physical. This is now a lesson in paying attention. It is a lesson in subjective versus objective data. Going back to when I first applied for my physical, there was a part of the paperwork that I filled out that had a page, front and back, with all kinds of "have you ever had or do you have" things, like asthma, heart disease, both eyes, birth control, stomach problems, psychiatric problems, foot problems, etc. There were two little boxes to check for each: "yes" or "no." When it asked me about foot problems, I didn't check either box. I was a nursing student after all and had taken anatomy and physiology. The "foot" did not constitute the "ankle." The nurse that came in and checked all my paperwork agreed with me, only she filled in the "no" box. She didn't write anything in noting my ankle injuries, because to her and me, I didn't have foot problems. This I distinctly remember. Now, in North Carolina, the same thing was happening. You needed to fill out all the paperwork all over again. I did the exact same thing. When the nurse checking me on the papers, got to the blank section she asked me, and I told her that I had had an ankle injury to each of my ankles. She noted it next to the box and checked "yes." You proceed from the papers to an exam, head to foot, inside and out. The army checks to see how physically fit you are to enter this advanced camp. If you pass, you go on to qualify for your commission. I remember entering one room where about twelve of us lined up on lines, both feet side by side, stand straight. There were evaluators walking around the room checking each of us for flat feet, bowed knees, posture, etc. I apparently did not pass muster, because they pulled another girl and me out of the pack and sent us into a different line. We were moving on to podiatry and orthopedic specialty exams we were told. There they poked, prodded, measured, pulled and evaluated both feet, knees, and ankles! They even took X-rays. While waiting, I kept wondering why they didn't do this when selecting for a scholarship. I think I was in and out in less than thirty minutes when I went to the clinic back in Vermont. The doctor came in and indicated to me that "I had an unfit left knee, had really flat feet, and an unfit ankle." He went on to tell me that the feet could be corrected with orthotics that I would wear in my shoes, but the knee and ankle would require surgery. I had a few choices. One, I could get the operation (by a military doctor) and come back for camp when I was fit; two, I could get a waiver and complete the training; or three, I could get out. I had a little bit of time to think about it, but I would bypass all the other parts of the exam and head back to the barracks. The other girl and I (I did not recognize her or know her because she was not in my company or barracks) got bussed back to the women's part of the barracks. (The "barracks" in the military is where we were all housed. A "company" was the group you got put in, divided into sections, where the whole group was made of companies called a battalion.)

I sat on my bed thinking. What I really wanted to do was just get out. I had been around military surgeons after splitting my eye open on a big wheel race when we lived in Virginia. The plastic surgeon was a military doctor who did not speak English. He stitched me up and I have a nice scar under my left eyebrow to this day. I thought about the nursing student back at UVM who had the same thing happen to her the year before. The doctor REALLY damaged her. She was still on crutches and considered "medical" for all the physical requirements. She was having a hard time doing clinical, because she couldn't stand for long periods of time and now walked with a cane. My decision was the third option. I was not going the surgical route. I had a weak ankle from turning it on that FTX, and if I couldn't get the scores on my PT test, or couldn't go fast enough on the land navigation, I would have to do this all over anyway I thought. For the first time I could remember, I prayed for some guidance. I had not really needed to pray about anything other than passing exams. I felt like I was being driven in my thoughts and made my decision.

I would opt out. *Only one thing left to do*, I thought. I have to tell my father.

I called my dad and briefly told him what had happened and what decisions needed to be made. I expressed my concerns for each. My father was dead set against me leaving. I was not getting any support for this decision. I hung up after telling him I needed to think. A female Major was being so nice to me, counseling me on these options. I expressed to her what my thoughts were. I went back to the barracks. About an hour later I got called back to the Major's office. "I just got off the phone with Colonel Krause, and he would like you to stay here," she said. She continued on and on about how great a person my father was and she, of course, knew someone who knew my father, etc. I told her that I knew my father was a great person, but ultimately it was my decision to make.

After sleeping on it for a night I really was set in my mind, I would opt out. I phoned my dad. "Dad, I am electing to get out at this point. I am comfortable with my decision."

"Heidi, I am telling you that you need to stay there at camp. I've arranged through the Major to make arrangements for you. You Do Not Want to leave," he said with exclamation. I could envision his most stern face, pursed lips, eyebrows raised, anger in his voice. When I was younger instead of a spanking, all my father had to do was raise his eyebrow and his cheeks would get really taut and I would burst into tears and submit.

"Dad, I have made my decision. I love you and I will call you when I get home," I said and hung up. This was the first time I had ever stood up to my father with MY decision, a grown up decision, regarding my life, not his. My dad did not speak to me for what seemed like weeks.

I was so glad to have Jerry home that I let the issue drop for now.

The weeks went by quickly. It seemed that even though Jerry was in school and I was working, it was as though we were already married. I saw him every morning and every evening. I still saw that look in Jerry's eyes and there were times when he would call his mom and dad and you could tell he was keeping something from them. Near Jerry's birthday, November 8, I answered the phone and on the other line was Jerry's mother. She had not heard whether Jerry had received the cake that she had asked one of the local bakers to make and deliver. The Baker indicated he delivered it to "my" house. The conversation seemed strained with Jerry, like he had been caught with his hand in the cookie jar. I learned soon after that his mom and dad had tried to contact him at school and hadn't spoken to him for over a week, so they tracked him down to wish him a happy birthday. Instead, they found him with me. As it turned out, the plan (according to Jerry's account) was that he would come back to school and see other women. His parents had hoped that he would see many girls and not, therefore, want to settle down and marry me. To them, as Jerry mentioned to me, I was Jerry's first real girlfriend. Jerry had never shared with them the many, many girls he had in fact been with. As Jerry put it "Dad told me to sow many seeds and hope for a lot of crop failures." Jerry had shared with me that some of his classmates' mothers had spent some time alone with him.... They never knew that.

Jerry was in fact relieved that I now knew the lie he was living to please his family.

That night, several of Jerry's classmates, Heather, Mike, Mark, Randy, and I witnessed the most spectacular show of the northern lights (Aurora Borealis). I had never seen the northern lights show so many vivid colors. What a great gift for Jerry's birthday.

Christmas vacation came and Jerry left to go home. According to his mother, it would be probably the last time they could celebrate as a family.

On December 23, the phone rang. Jerry was on the phone. "I'm at the airport in Dayton. Can you come and get me at the Burlington airport in a couple of hours?" He didn't say why or sound very good. When I picked him up at the airport, I was silent and listened to him in tears tell me that his family had set him around the table and had a "family meeting" to discuss why he had not broken up with me. His family was not going to let him come back to Norwich for his last semester and at that point had him make a choice of what he wanted to do. He said he was going to finish at Norwich and he was going to marry me. His family told him that if that was his choice they would no longer pay for him to come to school, he was "on his own." They told him he could not stay in their home. He went to his grandparent's house, where Bampa told him he could stay and then wound up giving him money for a plane ticket back to Vermont. I listened, let Jerry cry, sob, yell, and carry on most of the way home. When we got home, my Dad and stepmother hugged Jerry and said he was welcome to stay. They didn't barrage Jerry with questions or give him a set of rules to live by. They did listen to his accounting of what had happened at his home.

The next couple of months, we went on planning for Jerry's graduation and our wedding. We continued with our Pre-Cana marriage preparation within the Catholic Church with Father Lavalley. Father Lavalley also counseled Jerry, as Jerry was having a hard time with his family's sudden ostracism. They had been very close. Jerry was drinking a lot and that worried me. Having seen my mother abuse alcohol and then watched her waste away, I knew it was not a healthy way to cope. I remembered again what the school counselor had once told me about the cycle of substance abuse. I had to trust that Father Lavalley would guide him. After about six weeks of counseling with Father Lavalley, Jerry backed off on the alcohol and started getting back to himself. He had not heard from his family. Father Lavalley did take me aside and tell me that Jerry's family had contacted him and as he told me they tried to tell him all the bad things about Jerry and about me. In regards to me, he told me that they had said to him that I wasn't Catholic enough. When I received my confirmation, Father Lavalley told me "I was as Catholic as the Pope." About a month before graduation, my father and stepmother got a call from Jerry's parents trying to "assassinate their own son's character," as my Dad told Jerry later. Two weeks from the wedding (which was scheduled for two days prior to graduation), Jerry's parents called the house and asked Jerry to reconsider. When Jerry told me about the conversation later, he told me that they had said that they could accept that he was going to marry me, but would we consider doing it one to two years later. Jerry firmly and confidently said no. They told him that since he chose not to put off the wedding, they would not be attending the wedding or graduation. This was just simply not fair. We did discuss putting the wedding off to a later date. Jerry was adamant that there was never going to be a good time for his family. They were how they were. He also thought that it made the most sense for everyone to travel for the graduation and the wedding. All of his friends and their families were around. We would have the wedding.

A week before the wedding, a package arrived in the mail. In the box was Jerry's letter jacket from school. A black and yellow jacket with an "O" for Oakwood High School and a framed picture of Alden Partridge Stamps (100) with the two parent buttons at the base of the matte, a note and bills for Jerry to pay for school.

The wedding was on a Thursday. Jerry's entire family was not there. Les's mother and father stood in as Jerry's parents. The wedding and the reception went off without any problems. Les and Art, Jimmy, Randy, Dave, Mike, and others all escorted us to our first night as man and wife. Neither of us had a clue where we were being taken. It was a surprise. While we were gone, according to my father, Jerry's mother called and wanted to talk with Jerry to tell him that his Bampa was in the hospital with a heart attack. My father told them he would get the name of the hospital and doctor to Jerry through his friends, because he did not know where we were. Jerry's mom hung up on him.

Graduation was a wonderful occasion and I was so proud of Jerry for working so hard to accomplish graduating on time. We were both in a wedding that day for two of his classmates in the corps (they had been in ours) and then the next day on to Stinson Lake in New Hampshire for a few days of fishing – me, our dog Panzer (a three-legged Rottweiler I had adopted from a patient), Les, Jimmy, and Art – on our honeymoon! We fished, cooked our own fish, hiked, and relaxed in the New Hampshire Mountains. The guys, who I had famously nicknamed the "Rat Pack," were such a nice crew. The Rat Pack had four others who weren't on this trip: Mike, Randy, David, and Peter. They were all so much like brothers. Art and Les had just gotten commissioned in the

Marine Corps and Jimmy in the Army. Jerry was going into the reserves. All of them wanted to spend this last week before going in to the "real" world. We fished and hiked, sat around and told stories about the fish we caught. I was really just one of the boys, not on my honeymoon, but I didn't care. All of us would be leaving within the next couple of weeks for destinations around the country. Jerry would be leaving for the School of Infantry for another six weeks and then Machine Gunner's school. I would not see Jerry for six weeks, join him for a weekend, and then he would be gone for another six weeks. He would then come home and start guard once a month. We stayed at Les's parent's house the night before Jerry left. He was the first of the Rat Pack crew to leave. He was throwing up all night before he left, he was so nervous.

When I went to visit Jerry in North Carolina, the main purpose of my trip, according to Jerry, was to conceive a child. Going to church the Sunday I was there, the message was from Genesis 18:11-14. The message essentially was that God blessed Abraham and Sarah, already old and barren. The end sentence caught my ear. "I will visit you this time next year and Sarah will have a son." The power of the Lord was working with me. I just knew I would be pregnant and that I would have a son. I prayed I was pregnant and I prayed for Jerry, as I knew he wanted so badly to be a dad. He had many happy memories of his childhood.

I WAS pregnant and was 8 weeks pregnant by the time Jerry returned. I was nauseated ALL the time. I was going in later to work, having shifted to working for the Gifford Home Health in Randolph. I had to stay later, but it wasn't too bad. At nine weeks, I was putting on my shorts, when a sharp pain doubled me over. Jerry took me to the ER. I was diagnosed with appendicitis and there was a danger I would lose the baby. I remember how mad Jerry was at the surgeon for saying it was likely I would lose the baby, but I would have many more opportunities. I had my appendix out under the watchful eye of my obstetrician. I can still feel the air in my shoulders from the air they blow you full of while under an epidural laparoscopy.

We waited for six weeks to make sure I would carry. When I finished my 16th week, we really got excited about having a baby.

At 30 weeks, Jerry's parents began calling and talking to Jerry again. He excitedly told them they would soon be grandparents. They all seemed genuinely happy and were even willing to accept me in to their lives. Jerry was working for a radio station in Montpelier and had begun to work with a man in Groton who sold life insurance. Jerry's dad sold the same kind in Ohio. It was a company called Modern Woodmen of America, a fraternal insurance company. Jerry worked so hard studying and was very determined to make this his new focus.

At 35½ weeks, I came home; a seemingly, normal day. Jerry was home, unusual for him. He showed me the pink slip from the radio station he had gotten earlier that day. "Now what will we do. You are going on maternity leave soon and I don't have two pennies to rub together." I figured Jerry would be hearing any day from Norwich as to whether or not he would be getting a newly created position called sports information director. Jerry had met several times with the public relations director and was told he basically had the job.

A few days later I came home, excited because my dad was coming up and Art, Jerry's school buddy, was coming up on some leave to visit. I walked in the door, and Jerry who normally is a very good communicator said "I am leaving for Ohio for some job interviews."

"When?" I asked.

"Tomorrow," Jerry stated.

"Why? I am not moving to Ohio. I am having a baby any day. I don't understand."

"There is this radio station in Cincinnati. I'm also going to meet with dad's boss Mr. Zellar," Jerry explained.

"But Art is coming. He is coming to see you and my dad. And there's supposed to be a huge storm. The timing is terrible. " *I could tell I was just not getting anywhere.*

"I'M going because Art and dad **ARE** going to be here. I won't be gone long," he said.

"Don't bother coming back. I AM NOT moving to OHIO!" I said defiantly.

Well, Jerry left the next day and I was miserable. I was convinced that this was the end of our marriage, because well, Jerry was building a relationship back with his family. He had struck out on his own, setting into motion a series of events that we don't still understand. Jerry was Abraham from Genesis. Jerry was striking out into parts unknown traveling on God's will with faith. I, on the other hand, was comfortable living right where we were. I was also ALL UTERUS. It was ALL about me, was supposed to be all about me and the baby. I was a disaster. I was up all night, crying, mourning, deciding what I was going to do. I went to Father Lavalley, my dad, and Art, as well as Missy. They, of course, were mad at Jerry for leaving, regardless of the fact they understood his desire to provide for his family. My dad was livid that after all the times Jerry had confided in him, he had not spoken to him in regards to this. With all the stress I was feeling, I began having contractions and was told by my doctor I was in early labor. When I did speak with Jerry, he said I couldn't possibly be in labor because "HIS mother had had five children and she convinced him by her experience that the first child would always be late!" According to his mother, I was making it up to have Jerry come home and then be lambasted by my dad and everyone else. The paranoia was very evident. I was just as paranoid they were going to keep him and not let him come home. We were adults. On top of all the stress of Jerry being gone and me being in labor, there was the snow! It has come to be known as the blizzard of 1993. The snow out on my dad's deck was five feet high. Art, one of the noblest of men, saw that my dad had to get back to DC and I was a mess emotionally, so he extended his leave time. The cleanup from the snow had been completed. Art was a godsend. Having someone to talk to was good also, since all I did was cry all night in between writing what I was feeling and then getting up from very uncomfortable sleep only to go to work.

At work I was able to see patients to keep my mind off my *dreaded* life of perceived single motherhood. However, I was resolved to make everything work. Friday of the following week, Jerry was scheduled to come home. Jerry's parents, who still didn't believe that my dad wasn't going to kill Jerry when he returned, were coming with Jerry to lend moral support. If need be, Jerry told me that he would return with his parents to Ohio. Since my dad had returned to Washington, DC, and Art was not going to get in the way of what should really be my relationship with my husband, my sister and her husband Bill would come up and be my support. Meanwhile, Friday morning, I went into the bathroom to find signs that I would be going into more active labor very soon. Contractions came every 15 minutes and were distracting enough that I would have to concentrate on my breathing. I still went to work, though, and my supervisor had me put my feet up – where she could watch me – and she knew the one place I could be reassured was at work.

I went home early to meet my husband and his parents. I really resented that he was bringing his mother and father to our meeting, but his parents demonstrated they really didn't trust their daughter-in-law or my father not somehow to meet with Jerry. My sister and her husband Bill were waiting at the house. Jerry and his mother, father, and sister Laura arrived shortly after. We met downstairs. It was very awkward to kiss my husband and greet him with such discomfort. Jerry's parents kind of looked around expecting my father to jump out. My sister and Bill greeted them, having never met before. They sat with me on the couch, and Jerry and his family sat opposite around the round oak table in our small apartment. I do not remember a thing about the conversation, only that I continued to have contractions through the whole time. It lasted a couple of hours, and when Jerry's mother felt all was well, Jerry told me he would take them back to the hotel, settle them in, and come home. I knew he was being respectful of them; however, knowing the ordeal was tough on me, I would have thought he would have let them go on. After all the verse says "a man shall leave his mother and father and cleave to the woman".

Jerry left, my sister and Bill left, and I sat, dissolving the ill taste in my mouth from this experience. Jerry called about thirty minutes later and said his parents were cleaning up and would attempt to drive back to Ohio. They would stay in Syracuse that night and continue on. He said he would get something to eat for us and be home soon.

Jerry arrived home with Gyro's, one of my favorites. Spiced lamb in a pita with onion and tzatziki sauce from a local restaurant in town was always an awesome treat. Since I hadn't eaten much in the last few days, we ate in silence, me stopping every once in a while to breathe through a moment of contraction. Jerry didn't seem to pay much attention. I did not finish my meal and felt I finally needed to lie down. Jerry and I decided we should talk, just the two of us, and it was OK if I lay on the couch. Not a moment into the conversation, I jumped up and ran to the bathroom. Jerry with a sarcastic tone of voice asked what was wrong. I asked for the phone and called my friend, Missy.

"Missy, what does it feel like when your water breaks?" I asked.

I was a maternal child health nurse, who spoke all the time of labor, delivery, and care of the newborn, yet all this knowledge went completely out the window when it came to me.

"If your water breaks your underwear doesn't smell," Missy said. I checked, and confirmed her instruction, and called the doctor. My water had broken and my contractions were getting stronger and closer. The doctor told me to come down to the hospital.

On we went, arguing the whole way as I had told Jerry I was in labor and Jerry was just not ready for a baby to come. I was three weeks early!!! His mother had told me and him that I would not go early. The stress of this past week was taking its toll, as I really couldn't concentrate.

I remember walking up and down the hallways discussing names. We had thought of plenty of boys' names but not for girls on the off chance I should have a girl. I delivered a six pound nine boy after about seven hours of active labor. For some reason, our baby left with Jerry to go to the nursery to be weighed and cleaned. They came back and our baby had a name! While in the nursery Jerry named our son, Gerald Louis III. Although it was after my husband, I hadn't thought we had actually decided on a name. I guess he looked like a Jerry and I wanted to honor my husband. I listened as Jerry contacted my Dad, his parents (who needed to continue on so Jerry's father could return to work), my sister, our friends, and anyone else he could think of. He was so proud of our little Jerry.

My family all came to see Jerry III, as well as Les's parents, Art, Randy, Mike, and the rest of my friends in the area. Art stood at the end of the bed, petrified to hold Jerry III, as he was afraid to drop him.

Well, I gave in to my husband's wishes, as the spiritual head of our household and we picked up and moved to Ohio. The words echoed in my ears from my mother, *make the best of any situation.* After all, Jerry had said "just until I learn the ropes, then I can come back and take over for Mr. Puffer when he retires. I can't wait to get some property on Winch Hill and we can build." I rationalized "at least it wouldn't be forever." We moved about three miles from Jerry's parents and started our lives in Centerville, Ohio. I was initially miserable, but determined to make the most of it. I made friends at the apartment complex we lived at and eventually with the neighbors. I started working back in homecare. It was there I met a wonderful bunch of women. We lived at the Villager complex. In a respectful, familial way, it was like a little soap opera at the Villager. Most of the units were single floor. Our apartment was an end unit in the back of this complex. It was quiet, set off of the street, with a row of brush and trees in front of our back yard, buffering the main street called Far Hills Road, the library, and some banks on the other side. A little stream trickled in front of the trees. A very small patch of grass allowed Jerry or me to take the two dogs out to play if we only had a few minutes. Otherwise we put them on their leashes and took them for a walk or to Caesars Creek. The apartment had two bedrooms, two baths, a fireplace, a kitchen, and a dining room. In the next building over, in another end unit, were friends of ours with two girls, Jessica and infant Michaela. Michaela was born on November 8, the same day as Jerry. Jeanne and Michael made Jerry Michaela's godfather.

On many occasions we went camping with them. Michael, who had a hearing impairment and wore an implant, was very computer savvy and he and Jerry enjoyed sharing a beer as well as liking camping. On one very hot July weekend, we trekked to camp within a couple hours from us in Kentucky. There was a lake and I remember swimming and getting very little relief. You could feel the humidity and Jeanne and I knew we would get a storm later. Our campground site was on a slope. We parked uphill and had to set our tent on the most level area we could find (it probably would have been better if we had put the tent where the cars were). Jerry, being the "Marine," pulled out his trowel shovel and began digging around the tent. Michael asked him what he was doing and Jerry told him in case of rain it was important to dig a trench around the tent so water didn't come in. Michael told him it was stupid and a waste of his time, so Jerry stopped. As the evening wore on, Jeanne and I went and bathed the two children, Jerry III and Jessica in the campground bathroom. We could hear the rumbling of thunder in the distance as we got back to the campground. As soon as it got dark, the skies opened up and the rain poured down. The six of us went into our tent and waited for the rain to stop. It didn't. I noticed after a few minutes my bottom was getting wet. I jumped up to see one of Jerry III's clean diapers I had tucked for quick use under his playpen/bed inside the tent, float towards me. Jerry started to chuckle and said something to Michael about the trench.... It was like something out of a movie as we dashed in between lightning bolts to our van, where at the time we had

Panzer our dog, nice and dry. We spent the rest of the night in the van "camping." I remember thinking this was not like the camping my family did and we did a lot of camping just about every weekend when we had lived in California while I was a child. I liked Jerry's mother's idea of camping (hotel-bound) much better.

Initially I got a job working for a home care company while Jerry began the very difficult job of building a client base of life insurance. Jerry had worked very hard on building his clients through Modern Woodmen. The type of visiting nursing I did involved a contract which I did not initially understand. I thought I was working an eight o-clock to four thirty day. Jerry III was in day care. With the particular contract I was responsible for, typically patients could be discharged at four in the afternoon and that would leave me with no daycare because Jerry had mostly evening calls to make in homes. I was miserable, cried mostly every day trying to make my job and my life in Centerville with my husband and son work, while making the most of it. Finally it was my husband who had had enough of me encouraged me to actually quit-a first for me. So I did. I started putting out resumes immediately for other home care/visiting nursing jobs as well. There were many competing companies in the Dayton, Ohio area.

The life insurance business was a struggle. Within the insurance field, you would make so many sales calls and few of those calls would lead to sales. If people bought, you got a bonus. If they didn't pay their premium, you got docked. Initially, Jerry got a paycheck with a consistent amount of money, but then it was just based on sales and there were a couple of months we literally got checks for $1.70! We lived off credit cards. I did laundry in the bathtub, so we could get diapers. Jerry would not let me apply for any assistance. He would tell me how bad that made him feel – "like he couldn't provide for his family." After about a year we were coming out of the hole, as my job was then full-time, after a few months of not working except in a "baby daycare" getting minimum wage while I waited for what I had heard was going to be a home care job at Kettering Medical Center Home Care. Frequently we would go look at houses we noticed in the area for sale. One day I brought up the question about moving back to Vermont.

"I thought you were going to learn the business and then move back to Vermont and take over for Harold, the district manager in Groton?" I asked.

"Well, honeyness, I have all these clients here now. I can't just leave them and go back and start over. We can get a second home and go there and retire" he replied.

That's it. I'm trapped. I thought I was being a trooper. I sooo missed Vermont, its mountains … my ability to see storms coming.

During this time I had a frequent reoccurring dream of a man without a face popping his head up in the picture window off of our dining room. It would wake me up in chills and crying. Jerry would wake up and ask me if I was okay and I would go back to sleep. I knew it was a man and I never saw the whole body, but just the upper torso. No features to a face, no words ever uttered. It was usually through the picture window; as I would peer out it the faceless being would just be there.

It was February and Jerry, Patrick, young Jerry and I traveled back to Vermont for Les's wedding. Les was the best man at our wedding and he was marrying back in New Hampshire. So, Jerry, Art, Jimmie, and Les would be back together. They were a great family. All of them had their idiosyncrasies. We also decided to get another Rottweiler puppy, because our three-legged Rottweiler, Panzer was beginning to show signs of extreme pain due to his constant "one-arm pushup" walking motion. Jerry had wanted to have the puppy around to learn some of the absolute best lessons of having an aged dog around. Later in the spring, we would ride back to Vermont and put Panzer down on Winch Hill. Jerry said on the ride that he would like to be buried on Winch Hill overlooking the world. "I want to be cremated and just put me up on the hill next to Panzer and your mom and Father Sutfin. I just know that if I am in some cemetery that eventually it won't matter who visits, some person will just move me or the stone and resell the plot, or imagine a great big flood coming and the cemetery flooding and all the coffins coming out of the ground." How ridiculous, I thought. Jerry and Art sat in the front driving to the wedding. Seeing the back of their heads and them bopping around back and forth doing motions to the song "Witchcraft" by Frank Sinatra in tandem, I was reminded how they resembled Ernie and Bert from Sesame Street. They hadn't seen each other in a bit and I marveled at how well they picked up where they had left off before we moved to Ohio.

Home from the White Mountains of New Hampshire, Jerry found some Yuengling beer while celebrating Saint Patrick's Day and sent a six pack to Les, Art, and Jimmy. He sat and drank the other six, sharing one with me celebrating that his son was turning two the next day on March 20. He had some work to do at home and his Delta 88 needed new brakes, so he stayed home Monday. He was going to take the two dogs to Caesars Creek to run around and play with our new two year old Jerry.

On Tuesday, March 21, I was driving my van home after a long day of orienting one of the new nurses. Our homecare agency had grown so much since I had started. I had done some of the paperwork earlier in the apartment and then progressed to doing visits with my mentee. Coming down Marshall Avenue, listening to the radio, I half heard a traffic report and the local news. There had been a very large traffic backup on I-75 South with apparent fatalities. I very briefly thought of Jerry and his father traveling from Toledo and that I hadn't gotten a message from Jerry like usual mid-afternoon. I briefly prayed for whomever was involved. I pulled in to my home and went next door to pick up Jerry III. I walked with the newest two year old Jerry III the twenty-five feet to the next building and opened the door. UGH! The smell was horrible. The two dogs – Panzer our three-legged Rottweiler and Kaiser the puppy – had gotten out of the kitchen and made a mess all over the off-white carpets! I did not hesitate to be angry with Jerry. Where was he? He hadn't been home to take the dogs out mid-afternoon.

I cleaned up the mess, grabbed their leashes, put Jerry in his stroller and took off on a walk. We walked our normal route, with me thinking of what I would say to my husband when he came home. Walking around to the parking lot, I didn't see Jerry's car. I was angry again. I noticed a police car parked in the lot where Jerry usually parked near my building and immediately thought the teen next door was in big trouble again. I rounded the sidewalk towards my entrance and there were indeed two policemen standing there. I said hello and one of them stepped towards me and asked if I was Heidi DuChene. I said "yes" and they asked if they could come in. My stomach really hurt. They wanted me to sit and I didn't want to. A flash of something from the radio and a fatal accident played back in my head and my prayer for the families. The policemen said there had been an accident and that Jerry and his dad had been killed. I was one of the families. God help me now.

What a blur as I sunk in to that deep cold water, struggling to get air from my crushing chest, listening as they asked if there was anyone they could call. I asked them to call Jeanne from next door to come over. The police indicated the accident occurred in the southbound lane while traffic was stopped because of an accident in the northbound lane and that folks were looking at that. A fourteen-ton truck came upon the three lanes of stopped traffic, apparently didn't stop, but somehow landed on top of the car, crushing my husband and father-in-law. I had visions of the horror. *Did Jerry watch the truck coming from his rearview mirror? What would I do?*

The phone rang; it was "Mom" (Jerry's mom) wanting me to come right over. I said I would be over soon. The officers offered to drive me, but I think Jeanne drove me. Again it was a blur, as we just sat in disbelief. People were stopping over. I didn't want to be there. I wanted to call **my** dad, **my** sister, **my** friends, Jerry's friends, my co-workers. I remember a call coming in while sitting in silence and Mom answering it. It was the organ and tissue procurement center asking if Jerry was an organ donor. I remember her saying that neither of the two were. I left, going home although I can't remember how I got home, to an empty home – quiet, lonely, dark. Jeanne was there and she wasn't leaving. She would sit with me until my parents arrived.

Somehow I don't remember talking to them, but they were coming. My friends Jean, Sonia, Sara, Kimmie, and Kellie were all trying to come. Gary, Les, Jimmie, Mike, and Randy from all over the globe were headed to Ohio. *As I sat – lost, drowning – I recalled the conversation just one month ago about Jerry's wishes. Had he somehow known?*

Now, I needed to fulfill those wishes for Jerry.

That night, I barely slept. My parents were on their way. Jeanne from next door was in the living room. I was so tired that I must have fallen immediately to sleep. At the right side of the bed (I slept on the right side of the bed), my husband in his tan/khaki suit was standing there, not on the floor, but slightly up, as if he was standing on the corner of the bed.

"Honey, I was in a terrible accident!" I shot up in bed and hoping it had all been a dream realized once more that my husband had died. Tears flowed again, as I cried until I couldn't cry anymore.

I wanted proof of Jerry's death. I needed to see his body. I somehow needed to trust that my in-laws had not come up with this scheme to take Jerry away from me. Jerry's mom wanted to bury Jerry and from conversations we had had ironically a month before at Les and Amy's wedding, Jerry wanted to be cremated and be placed on "the hill" – Winch Hill, where we were living at my parent's house. Jerry's mom had already bought a plot at the cemetery for herself, her husband, Jerry, and Laura. I remember her pleading to keep Jerry with his family. My conspiracy thoughts had been that somehow she was in cahoots with the funeral director and I would be duped like in thriller movies; yet knowing this was more like a reality show. I also had feelings of disbelief that this had happened at all, that in true Jerry fashion he would walk through the door in a dramatic entry. Initially, though, at the church there would be caskets and the wake would be open-casket. You know, I really would never wish this for me or for my family. Put me in the cheapest pine box and cremate me. I'm not there; I am with Jesus. Anyway, my dad tells me that the funeral director strongly urged me not to view Jerry's body and truthfully, I don't remember seeing the body of my husband there, but I remember being convinced. I still have Jerry's Norwich ring, his glasses splattered with a combination of his body fluids and those of the car and his wallet in my strong box to this day. I took his wedding ring from the bag and placed it on my ring finger next to my wedding ring and engagement ring (Jerry had given me it after we were married, along with a mini Norwich ring.)

The accident occurred in the afternoon of March 21. Traffic had been backed up on Dayton I-75 northbound for an accident and Jerry and his father were literally parked in the southbound lane, three lanes near the Needmore Road Exit. A fourteen-ton, white Mack truck essentially drove over the top of Jerry's maroon-colored Delta 88, crushing both Jerry and his father from above. Both were wearing seatbelts and to this day, I wonder if either saw the truck bearing down on them. I wonder their thoughts.

There was one witness who wrote me – I can't find the letters right now – who said that Jerry lived for a little while and he held his hand while help rushed to the scene. He wanted me to know that Jerry wasn't alone. Another witness says that he was walking over the overpass and witnessed this truck not even slowing down for traffic on a clear day, hitting one car before "popping" onto Jerry's vehicle. Having not been at the scene, I felt I needed to see my husband with my own eyes. Apparently I was convinced.

Psalm 91:11 says, "For He shall give his angels charge over you, to keep you in all your ways." I was standing at the kitchen sink of our apartment, just blankly thinking, talking to myself, and talking to my husband Jerry. "I just hate having to take out the garbage. This was something that you did. I hate putting away the socks you leave strewn about when you walk in the door taking off your shoes, leaving them there, taking off your tie, leaving it on the couch, socks, then shirt, then pants, oh… those got to the floor of the bedroom…" I stopped. There was a noisy chatter coming from outside the window.

"Dit dit dit dit dit dit dit." And it stopped. I listened. "Dit dit dit dit dit dit dit." Where was that coming from? I looked out the window. Sitting about fifteen yards from me, bright and colorfully red, was a cardinal. I said "Hello." It started again: "Dit dit dit dit dit dit dit." It stopped. I felt comfort in that moment. I grabbed the garbage and started around our building (we were in the end unit). The cardinal didn't move. It just stayed there. I walked past it with the garbage, and it started: "Dit dit dit dit dit dit dit," again. And then it flew right past me to the tree by the garbage container in the parking lot. I dumped the garbage and turned to walk back. The bird flew past me again and right to the post on the tree it had left a few moments ago. In that moment, it was the bird and me and I felt an overwhelming sense of peace as though Jerry were there chastising me and I really don't care if anyone thinks I am crazy. At my age, why isn't this crazy? I somehow knew though that things would be okay. The cardinal came back and forth to the spot and chit chattered at me a couple of times a day for the next week.

The calling hours were unbelievable. There were people lined up around the block of the funeral home of Dayton, Ohio. Hours were from 4 to 8 and they had to extend them because so many people wanted to visit. There was a Knights of Columbus full contingent standing watch all the time because both Jerry and his father were fourth-degree knights. My stepmother (who I now called mom), Deb had taken an exhausted and slightly confused little Jerry III back to the apartment and I stayed, greeting well-wishers. I had been pregnant then – probably just only a couple of weeks – but the stress caused me to miscarry.

The church was huge. Jerry or his family had apparently belonged in the huge parish, which to me resembled a cathedral. I don't remember the whole actual funeral. I remember walking down the aisle slowly with my just turned two year old Jerry III holding my hand along with my parents. I was ushered into the second row. In the front sat Nanny, Jerry's mom Sharon, Patrick, Philip, and Laura. I sat on the outside of the left-hand side of the aisle. To my right, in the aisle way after people had been seated was Jerry's coffin, draped with an American flag. Both Jerry and his dad had been in the service. Jerry Sr. had served in the Air Force. He was in a band called "The Four Saints," which performed all over the world, including inaugural balls. I remember Jerry saying that he had sat on Dolly Parton's lap at the Grand Old Opry when his father had been on tour. Jerry had told me that he spent a lot of time with his Nanny and Bampa growing up early, as his dad was on tour. His father had been on the Ruth Lyons and Ed Sullivan shows, had made albums, and had even owned a hotel in Florida, where the band would go to play. He had also told me that prior to marrying his mother, Jerry's father had been married to an Englishwoman. They lived in Georgetown in DC and she died of cancer.

To my dad, it was maddening to have his daughter placed in behind "immediate" family, when I at least should have been in the front row, since my husband had died. He had words with the priest, something he would normally never do. I don't remember much of the funeral, except for how horrible it was to be my age and have to endure. My parents made mention of their distaste at what happened. Reflecting on it years later, it was just another example of irrationality that happens during bad situations

I remember Jerry and my friends being there, Randy, Mike, Gary, Mark, Les and his new wife Amy, Mike M., Dave, Jean, Sonia, and people from work, helping with the reception after the funeral.

"The lord watches over the alien and sustains the fatherless and the widow, be he frustrates the ways of the wicked" (Psalm 146:9).

So everyone gradually left and young Jerry III and I assumed our roles, with me going back to work and Jerry III going to Jeanne's house for daycare. I returned to work three weeks after the funeral. Being at work was busy. Life went on for everyone I was finding. People still needed me to do the things in their home that they couldn't do. I sat at my desk, which was a counter space cubicle. I had a filing cabinet and cork board in front of me on the wall for planning and I was coordinating other nurses, home health aides, and case management as a team leader for Kettering Medical Center Home Care. I needed to call a doctor and report findings on a patient. I dialed Dr. V and reached his nurse. I was patched through to the doctor. When I finished giving my report to the doctor, he said to me "you know Jerry lives on in others." Thinking about my son Jerry III, I said, "yes it was comforting to know that little Jerry was alive and I saw so much in him that reminded me of Jerry his dad." The doctor voluntarily said that my husband Jerry's corneas had been successfully donated and the recipient was doing exceptionally.

"Excuse me," I said, "my husband wasn't an organ donor."

The doctor went on, stammering slightly about something I didn't even hear, because I was in shock over what had just been said to me.

My mind flashed back again to the month before Jerry and his dad died…. Jerry and I were on our way to Les's house for a pre wedding dinner. It was February and cold, but very sunny. For some reason we began talking about organ donation. Jerry happened to believe that there was a "conspiracy" in the medical field and he felt that sometimes things happen and "your body isn't even cold" when doctors take out what they need and the survivors never know what has been harvested. He mentioned to me that he would **never** voluntarily donate his organs. Being a nurse, I believe in the benefits of organ transplantation. I hadn't really thought about people taking something that they knew would benefit someone else without permission … but after all, the person is dead. With Jerry's perspective it is like embezzlement. You don't know what you don't know. Now hearing from the doctor, Jerry's thought process kind of slammed me in the face. He was right!!!!! I just started sobbing, as I was grieving all over again, something I couldn't control – or could I?

I called my lawyers. I mentioned what had happened and my lawyer told us to get a good lawyer for a wrongful death suit. MaryEllen listened and offered some comfort in looking into it. I mentioned remembering being at my mother- in -laws and the call I overheard her say to the organ bank, "my husband and son were not organ donors," and declined for both of them. I called my mother-in-law and told her what had just happened. She was equally distraught. Later in the day, MaryEllen called back to tell me that it was perfectly legal for the procurement of corneas and pituitary gland tissue from my husband in Ohio. The law, called "presumed consent," allowed for the procurement of these tissues and it was presumed "okay" unless the survivor called and declined. *"Wow," I thought. "Do people know they have to do this?"* This was terrible and demonstrated even more how Jerry was right. I felt I needed to do something about this – for Jerry and all those that couldn't speak. I called WHIO, the Channel 3 CBS affiliate, with which I had worked recently in regards to home care. I asked to speak with John Condit. I told him what had happened and asked him if there was a possible story. He indicated his intrigue in all sides of the story. He agreed to do a story. In the meantime he put me in touch with the local legislator, Mike Drinkwine, and suggested I talk to him. This law needed to be changed. People needed to hear about it.

WHIO did a news investigation showing both sides of the issue. It was nicely done; the story was called "Presumed Consent." With their publicity and working with Mike Drinkwine, I was able to utilize my rights as a citizen and work with the legislative branch and get the presumed consent law changed. It had never been brought to the legislature, but the judicial branch had made it a statute. When I eventually moved back to Vermont, the very first thing I did was contact my legislators and determine that Vermont did not have a presumed consent law, but New York, New Hampshire, and Massachusetts do.

It was suggested that I go to a young widows support group. I was the youngest one there, being 27. The next youngest was in her late 30s. While I found that we had death of a spouse in common, I just didn't feel comforted by this group. I found that my co-workers and my extended Northfield and Norwich family made a point to come and visit me. Michael, Randy, and David from Jerry's Rat Pack visited often. Randy was in the 82nd airborne, based out of North Carolina. Randy loved our Rottweiler and this inspired him to get one. When he went out in the field, he would bring "Nikki" to me to take care of. She got along quite well with the other two and I worked on training her in addition to Kaiser.

Church was also comforting to me. I did not "belong to a church," but went with Jerry III up the street to a Catholic Church to which our little family had started to go. I found the structure of going made me feel better, finding solace in knowing God was with me and even that Jerry's spirit was with me somehow, in my heart. We had attended this same church together and it was comforting to know that. I still had so many questions for God. Why? Not just why, but the true fear, was Jerry wondering what I was doing? Was he with me or was he with God?

I fear death and wonder what happens after death. I also fear being forgotten. I want to be known, to leave a mark on the world. I had to have faith in knowing at least that I would live on with family through a couple of generations. So, I committed myself to having the faith and courage to grab a hold of that to carry me wherever God needed me to be.

The "Why?" remains pretty common for anyone who has lost a loved one at ANY point in life. I somehow had to come to grips with just letting go of something I could not control, knowing that God would help us use my suffering to strengthen me and glorify Him. "Consider it pure joy, my brothers, whenever you face trials of many kinds, because you know that the testing of your faith develops perseverance. Perseverance must finish its work so that you may be mature and complete, not lacking anything" (James 1:2-4). I continued to pray for the wisdom that would come from this suffering. I prayed that my mother's words of making the most of it and God's promises that He would NEVER leave me alone with my suffering meant that somehow I would grow and good would come out of this.

The man that ran over my husband had had his commercial driver's license suspended in North Carolina, but still was able to get a job driving a truck in Ohio. The trucking company was a small operation called City Trucking. The driver, Howard Lindsay, Jr., was charged with vehicular homicide. He was cited to appear in court and did not show for court for his pretrial several times, so an arrest warrant was issued for him. The charge if convicted of vehicular manslaughter was at least six months in jail per incident. This was the same as the penalty for littering in Dayton area. How utterly unfair, but also pretty common all over the country.

Honor

"To hold to the highest moral principle

in absence of strict conformity"

The one person who could not make Jerry's funeral was Art. Arthur was one of Jerry's best friends and a member of the Rat Pack – a silly group that really started out getting together over Rolling Rock or Yuengling beer and going to the local Rustic Restaurant for its famous cheeseburgers and fries. Art was there when I had Jerry III. He had even attended a childbirth class with my sister and me during the drama with Jerry being gone. Art was deploying to the Mediterranean for six months and could not get leave because Jerry wasn't a blood relative. I remember speaking to him on the phone, how hard it was for him to talk and how much he wanted to be around for Jerry and me. He began writing me every day, logging his trip, and I returned the letters, journaling through my grief. He called just about every week when he was in port. Eventually, the letters began to be more revealing about his feelings for me and for Jerry and he declared his intentions to come back and take care of me. He wanted me in his life in a more romantic way. I had never thought of him in this way, because Jerry WAS my world. I found myself falling for him also. He was easy to talk with, he was away, and I was learning to be independent again, like when my mother died. Art was a political science major at Norwich. He was a genius. A "perfect Marine," six foot two, eyes of blue. He was in great shape and could have been the poster child for the Marines. He also went to Norwich University and was the corps of cadets' executive officer in his senior year (second in command). He embodied honor and integrity. He was also a Christian man who chose to be a virgin until he was married. I remember once while we still were in school the Rat Pack boys (Jerry, Les, Jimmy, Randy, Pete, Dave, and Mike) were at the Rustic. The subject of sex came up and the very close – infer too close – relationship that Art had with one of the assistant commandants – Maureen. The boys felt that Art must have been sleeping with her. Art was furious that his honor was in question. He left his Norwich Ring on the table and told them that if his word wasn't good enough then the ring meant nothing. He walked back to campus, three miles from the restaurant. The boys never spoke of it again and gave Art his ring back.

Art WAS always there for his best friends. I had NO idea that Art loved me from the moment he met me or that he compared any girl he met or dated to me, as he started to say in his letters. I didn't perceive he would ever cross a line and make a play for me. No wonder though. I thought that he had made a big effort to be there for me when Jerry was gone to Ohio while I literally labored. Art sent me pictures and beautiful knick knacks from the Mediterranean. He would share with me how much the "moral compass" that some of the officers had while in port bothered him. Some of his superiors were married and one of them was awaiting his fifth child and was going out to buy some pleasure (meaning prostitution). Condoms were handed out at check out from the boat. Art ranted like Jerry. Thinking back about the two of them, I recalled thinking they resembled Bert and Ernie from Sesame Street and that made me laugh. The two were passionate. When I talked with Art while he was stationed in the Mediterranean, the phone had a three second lag, so hearing him rant was sometimes even funnier, because it would be broken up or seem like no one was on the other end of the line. By June, his letters switched from friendly to more intimate. He told me he loved me and would I consider marrying him? I didn't believe what I read. What an honorable thing for Art to do, to make sure Jerry III had a father and I had a husband. I was very comfortable with Art: his soul was pure, moral, and full of value.

While I was in high school, I was in a rock band. It was called Special Projects in Music, because we got a grade and credit for it. One of my best guy friends in the band was Mark. I had a crush on him and during school there was a two week "flirt" where he would sit behind me in class and play with my hair or touch the small of my back, leaning to pass papers forward to the front of the class. He was off limits, though, at the time because of an insanely jealous girlfriend. When Jerry died, Mark was living in Michigan and after the funeral he would visit frequently. When he came to the funeral, he brought his girlfriend, Julie. The next time he visited he told me that Julie and he had broken up. Mark also went to Norwich and not only was I physically attracted to him, but he was also familiar, kind, and understanding. He was someone I could talk to about mature, adult things and I felt somewhat isolated now. He was a piece of home. On his visits, we would do family-type things. I could be myself. I did see that there could be more for us, but for some reason there was Art. *What was happening in my spirit?*

Dave, Randy, and Mike would visit also and it was nice taking a boisterous two year old Jerry III and the dogs out of the "house" and feeling somewhat normal. As I was learning to live with myself and with Jerry III, I learned to accept what had been somewhat of a norm at my household … people came and went. After all it was that way as I was growing up. We moved, we had people come, spend time with us, and they left. It was so important during this time for little Jerry to know how many people loved him. Keeping busy was also important and living in an apartment there was only so much cleaning we could do so it was great to have visitors.

Gerry D. was a friend of my husbands from elementary and high school. His dad was a doctor at Kettering and just before Jerry Jr. died, the two had reestablished contact. After the accident, Gerry was the one who, through his father, suggested to my father about contacting a law firm. He came over a lot and also declared that he wanted to make sure "little" Jerry had a father-figure in his life.

Gerry D. was also a salesman, but did not sell life insurance. Gerry sold gadgets, and products. Before my husband died, we bought a water purifier that attached to our tap from the sink, for "the best water, free of contaminants." When Jerry died, Gerry's latest sales "thing" was natural products and wanted to make sure to start me on these supplements, since I was under stress. Gerry D. was always around, but he was too much for me and tried way too hard to seem like Jerry. He wasn't for me. There was only one Jerry for me.

Over the summer, I travelled back to Vermont with the sole purpose of buying property with the life insurance money that my husband provided in death to me. I looked at many places in Northfield and I liked a couple. When Jerry and I had been living in Vermont, we would walk down the road from where we lived at my dad's. Jerry loved one house about a mile north from my Dad's that had a three hundred sixty degree view of the campus. It was owned by a family, Norma and Jack, with whom my mother and father were close. My mother was closer to Norma than my father and Norma was a recovering alcoholic. In fact, prior to my mother's death, my mom had intended to go to the same clinic where Norma had gone in Europe. Norma passed away shortly after Jerry III was born and Jack, Norma's husband, briefly re-married before he died. Jack and Norma had four children and some of them didn't live in the area. They decided they would auction off all the belongings of the home and sell the "ninety-five" +/- acres of property. I asked my friends David and Missy to look at the house for structure, as I couldn't be there to see it empty. I was already familiar with it, coming to Jack and

Norma's a lot in the summer and swimming in the pool along with the grandchildren. David and Missy brought my friend Mark, the engineer to see the property. Their opinion was that a lot of work would need to be done, but they advised me to make an offer. Originally the family did not take the offer. They wanted a lot and even with Jerry's life insurance, I couldn't afford it. I was disappointed. I told the realtor if the family decided to sell in two parcels, I would be interested in buying the land. The realtor, Paula, mentioned this to the family. I prayed they would split the property and I could buy the land. I got the call from Paula saying she had spoken to the family and mentioned how I used to live up the road and the family had not connected the last name until then with who I was. They agreed to split the property and sell the land to me. Ironically, they had also gotten an offer on the house as soon as word had gotten out.

September arrived and Art declared he would come to Ohio and we would all drive to Vermont for alumni weekend at Norwich. I would close on the property to which Jerry and I had dreamed of retiring. Art had plans to "ask my dad for my hand in marriage." *What would that walk be like?* I thought. My friend and co-worker Joy from Ohio and Gerry D. would also travel with us to Vermont.

I had worked with Joy. When Jerry was alive, he and I were convinced that Joy was absolutely perfect for Art. I tried to set them up a couple of times. They were cordial to each other, but never hit it off. Joy and I were close. We had lost our mothers very young and saw ourselves going in to healthcare for the same reasons – alcoholism in families, suicide, depression, etc. I oriented Joy to home healthcare. She had worked for the same hospital in cardiac rehabilitation, prior to coming to homecare. Joy was tall, slim, wore glasses, and even through those glasses her greenish blue eyes sparkled and she always seemed to have a smile on her face.

There is advice that comes with great wisdom. When a spouse dies or you go through a major change, it is recommended by "the powers that be" not to make any major decisions within a year. I was only partially thinking this pertained to me. Somehow I got talked into trading in my Dodge Caravan for a tricked-out van. It was really a camper on wheels, with TV and VHS player. The back seat of the van laid out into a bed. I bought it with the intention of going back and forth between Ohio and Vermont in comfort. There wasn't a lot of clearance and gas mileage wasn't terrific. At my homecare, I called the van my office. I would often park in the office's parking lot to do my paperwork. I sat out doing paperwork when OJ Simpson was found not guilty of the charge he killed his wife.

We were going to stay with Jim, another Rat Pack classmate. Jerry, Les, Art, and Jim's girlfriend and her son were coming. We would all stay in a condo in Sugarbush, a ski resort area about thirty miles from Norwich. The first night in Vermont, Art presented me with an engagement ring and I, so full of emotion, gave myself to him and we slept together. I am still not happy that we didn't wait until we were married, but I didn't think much about it. I needed to move forward without Jerry. During the weekend, we made plans for a wedding the following alumni weekend in the fall in Vermont. Art believed that he would leave the Marine Corps as he felt that the Marine Corps was not a place to raise a family. (*He and Jerry had at one point chuckled while saying in gruff drill sergeant voices, "If the Marines wanted you to have a wife they would have issued you one".*) We discussed building a home in Vermont and moving back. Art would apply for a job at Norwich.

During the weekend, our group walked up to the spot where Jerry wanted his remains to stay. We said some prayers and Jerry III and my niece Audrey placed roses on the stone. Art met with my father, declaring his love and intentions. He asked for my hand in marriage and the two walked the hill that my father and Jerry had walked previously. My dad shared the story of "the walk and shock" with Jerry and they visited the spot where Jerry's remains were set. Also during the weekend, we attended a ceremony at Norwich, placing Jerry's name on the school's "Harmon Wall." This wall was created with the intention to honor great alumni, faculty, staff, and friends of Norwich who contributed to the ideals of the university's mission, with service to others above self, bringing honor to the school. Jerry's name was engraved in granite under 1995.

Art came back to Ohio and stayed for three weeks. During this time I was tired, my breasts hurt. One day after coming home from work and falling asleep on the couch for a couple of hours, Art suggested, "Well, maybe you're pregnant."

"We only had that one time," I exclaimed, *knowing that he was right, nonetheless.* Of all the times I had been to patients' houses listening to them talk about getting pregnant on the pill or using a condom and saying the same thing, I had to laugh at myself. "*All it takes is one,*" my little voice said inside. I hadn't thought about protection or even sex with anyone other than my husband and with him having died, there was no need even to think about it. *What would Jerry's mom think?* I had been getting along so much better with Jerry's mother. We had had great conversations about relationships as she had pointed out that I spoke of Art often. I didn't want to break her heart by telling her that not a day went by that I didn't cry out to God inside how much I missed Jerry and wanted him back, but since that wouldn't happen and I was moving forward it was all I could do. I really wanted to share with her that Art had asked me to marry him. She would often talk about how she felt she could NEVER remarry. I definitely didn't want to hurt anyone's feelings. I took a pregnancy test and it was positive. Art was ecstatic. I was in a panic. We decided that we would get married in December, instead of the following year, and then I would move back to Vermont in January and Art would finish his assignment in North Carolina.

I had only met Art's mother and his aunt before graduation a couple of years before. Art's father, who was older than his mother, had passed away during Art's freshman year at Norwich. Art's mother, Joyce, and Aunt Clare drove up from Florida, where they lived.

Art's mother was tall, with very kind features. Her voice was quiet, but strong. She had been caring for her sister Clare, who had never married. Aunt Clare was very proud of Arthur (which is what Art's mother and family called him). They were used to all the snow in Vermont and the driving, as their whole family had grown up in Maine. They also had many relatives who lived in New Jersey. Art's father had been married before and had three children. Art's step-siblings were closer than most I have met. His brother David and his wife Patty had three children, which would make me an aunt. He had a sister, MaryAnn, who also had three children, who were closer in age to Art. Art told me that his oldest brother Stephen resembled his father the most. He was a great cook and ran a diner that his father had started. His brother Stephen and wife Poppy had three children who also were the same age as Art. Art's whole family was so welcoming and loving. Everyone immediately made me feel comfortable, the most perfect example of unconditional love I had seen. Everyone that came to the wedding was so happy for Art. Their joy for him having met his dream girl was humbling to me. For a wedding gift, Art gave me a set of earrings and a necklace made from diamonds that his Aunt Claire had given to him. The necklace was a chain with a gold pendant in the shape of an oak tree with diamonds filling in the spaces like the foliage. The earrings matched with a single diamond. He had designed it himself and had made at a local jeweler's.

Before Jerry III and I left Ohio to move back to Vermont, Jerry III, Jerry's mother, Patrick, Philip, Emily, and Laura, as well as Jerry D. and my friend Joy sat in the courtroom. Shortly before going into the courtroom, the probation and parole officer spoke with Jerry's mom and me. He told us that for the first time in this officer's career (over fifteen years) this offender had never even shown ANY kind of remorse, that his attitude was "well the world just has two less white guys in it." (Having never seen the man who killed my husband, I had not known he was black.) It was his recommendation to the court for the maximum sentence of the full year, because of "each incident," his ignoring the law by not showing up in court, and fear that he would go back to his home in Kentucky if only given probation and the court would not be able to extradite him. Sitting in the courtroom, Mr. Howard "L" stood in front of the bench. He made no motion, just stood facing the judge in a sweatshirt and jeans and handcuffs. Both Jerry's mom and I spoke to the court during the sentencing.

After the judge heard from us, he asked if Mr. Howard "L" wanted to address the court. He did not. The judge gave him the maximum sentence and Mr. Howard "L" finally turned and made eye contact with me for the first time. A chill went up the back of my spine as the "man without a face" from my dream suddenly met my gaze. The gaze burned through me. I felt as though if he hadn't been going to jail that look would have been threatening. My friend Joy asked me later if I had seen the way that man had looked at me. She had been right behind me and commented about how incredibly angry the gaze at me was. *I hadn't imagined it.* I was glad I would be moving to Vermont, to protect my precious son from this man who had devastated two families' lives.

In January, I moved back to Vermont and we moved all the furniture we could into the downstairs apartment at my parents, where I had lived with newborn Jerry and husband Jerry Jr. The land I had bought in September would be a great house site and together Art and I started planning for building in the spring. Art had not yet left the Marines. The Marines were having difficulty letting one of their best officers go. My father was using some of his influence to allow him to leave the service and Art would apply for an admissions position that our friend David had heard about at Norwich. We broke ground on the driveway in May and planned to move into our home in the fall. I don't know if you have ever built a house with anyone, but it was pretty clear to me that it would be a test of wills. Art was incredibly smart and extremely smart with money – almost too frugal at times. Instead of enlisting the help of an architect, we combed through books of designs that were already approved by architects with the three sets of plans needed for electrical, plumbing, etc. As he put it "we will be saving the 10% mark-up on the architect by taking our concept and finding a commensurate plan in a book for $500.00."

We already had a builder who was a partner of my father. Between him and Art, they would keep to budget and timing. Yet, it was still stressful, timing the money without getting a mortgage. A settlement had been reached with the company and lawyers from Jerry's wrongful death suit and the portion of the money I would get would build the house. It was very important to Art that we did not go in to debt. We took daily or weekly photos to journal the progress. I couldn't do a darn thing around the place because I was so pregnant and the builder didn't really want me around to do anything – not even pick up trash. I set my sights on cutting the pine trees that ran single file up and down the road. When I was growing up the owner of the property, which at the time ran along both sides of the road planted single red pines. Now that the east side of the road belonged to us, I thought they would look super if they were pruned from the ground up, uniformly six feet or so. One weekend, David and Art cut the tree branches exactly how I wanted and then as they grew into piles every fifty yards or so, they would burn the piles of limbs. David and Art were like kids. At least kids that liked to build and destroy with fire. Both of them were very proficient at lighting fires, but admittedly they made me nervous at their overconfidence when lighting – getting a little too close a couple of times and putting me at a watchful distance, deciding whether to call the fire department or an ambulance.

It was a great project and created the ability for cars to look up at the house and for us to see cars coming up the road. Once it was completed, the house looked massive from the road. David and Art came up with a great name, deciding the house would be called The Crow's Nest. When David, Art, and Jerry attended Norwich, David, who graduated in 1986, and Art, who graduated in 1992, would be at their mess hall. The upperclassmen or the officers holding rank in the corps would sit up higher in a section of the mess hall called the crow's nest. This allowed for the students who had rank to look out amongst the rest of the corps. Announcements would be made during the meal, which they called "mess." There were three messes for the three meals of the day. Our home had one of the most spectacular views looking out on the town, mountains; since it was facing south of town we could practically "do the traffic report from our porch". From a different perspective I also had a love for nautical things, sailboats. Knowing the top of the tallest mast of sailing vessels was called the crow's nest only seemed appropriate. The name fit perfectly.

Once I was back in Vermont, I wrote a letter to Jerry's mom explaining where I was coming from. I was a coward for not seeing her face to face. She wrote me back pretty much telling me that she was hurt and didn't understand, but that she had "heard through the grapevine" that I was getting remarried and she assumed it was Art that I was marrying. I had mixed feelings in my heart. After all, they hadn't attended their own son's wedding; why would they go to Art's and mine? Selfishly, I did not give them the opportunity to say yay or nay. I didn't want their rejection again, but I didn't even give them that chance. I should have. We had connected through the deaths of Jerry and his dad. The grapevine had been my big mouth, telling a woman in the nail salon where I was having my nail repaired before going to Vermont for the wedding. I had literally set my thumbnail on fire lighting a candle. I didn't know how flammable acrylic nails were and was happily sharing my news, but a friend of Jerry's mother overheard and told her. Although our relationship remained friendly and Jerry's mom continued to support and mentor me, I had really hurt her.

In June, on Flag Day, my water broke and it was time for the baby to be born. Art drove me down to the same hospital in which Jerry III was born. It seemed like yesterday, but it was three years earlier under different circumstances than this pregnancy and delivery. After a very painful labor and almost an emergency C-section, I delivered Michael Stephen. He weighed 9 pounds 6 ounces! He had been wedged inside me in what was called the posterior presentation (face up) and looked like a prizefighter when he first came out, bruised and swollen from all the pushing. Missy and David visited and my dad happened to arrive for a visit to see a new grandson, his namesake.

Later, in June, we received a final settlement from the wrongful death suit. It was divided into three parts, with lawyers receiving one third, me receiving one third, and the rest going to a trust to be determined by the probate court in Ohio for benefit of Jerry III. In Ohio, if a person dies without a will, as in other states, any awards to minors are administered through a probate court system. Money is placed into a trust – in this case a bank – and a trustee administers the trust for the benefit of the child. Art tried to make suggestions for where the trustee could put the funds. Art, being so frugal and a genius with money, once took a cash advance on a credit card when he graduated from Norwich. He took the cash advance, invested the money, made a profit, paid back the credit card without ever paying interest, and then used the money he gained as a day trader. I had to decide on the bank that would be the trustee for my child. It seemed silly since he was my child. The state of Ohio believed that it was in the best interest of a child to have an account started that would raise money. The court stipulates that the trustee can charge fees and administer the trust for the benefit of the child. I chose the PNC bank, because the trustee who would supervise Jerry III trust knew my father-in-law. He assured me that while the original amount was $133,000, by the time Jerry III turned 25, he would be a millionaire. He did not take any fees or charge for the accounting he had to do for the court. Initially Skip listened to Art's suggestions and worked with the two of us. Jerry's account blossomed to over $250,000 in a booming market over the next several months.

In September, I received a letter in the mail from the probation and diversion department in Ohio notifying me of Mr. Howard's potential release from jail for good behavior. The whole incident of sitting in the courtroom came back to me. How could this even be a possibility? For good behavior they would potentially turn this man's incarceration into probation. *In my opinion he should be in for life*, I thought, but the law said a maximum of six months per incident. I felt so threatened, even though I was in Vermont, because of the way this man's eyes pierced into me when he had turned around at the courtroom. I wrote a letter, as did Jerry's mom, and thankfully the judge ordered the maximum sentence to be completed.

We moved into our new home on October 14, 1996. I spent the first night in our home praying in thanks to the Lord for a roof over our heads. I also prayed that both the roof and the house would remain intact as the wind howled outside so fiercely. I didn't realize that on a hill in a field, the wind whipped from the Northwest from October to April and then shifted in the spring. I prayed my builder had known this when he constructed.

We had a housewarming party with many of our friends. My friend Joy had moved from Ohio and was living at my parents' home in the apartment Art and I had lived in, as well as Jerry and I when he was alive. She and I were working for a home health agency in Randolph, an exit south of our town but nineteen miles away. One of the guests, whose name is Bill Passalacqua, gave us the most amazing gift. It was a box with a bottle of wine, pasta, sauce, and a log and candle. The note written on the card had to do with the contents and much enjoyment in our home. "Place a log in the fire, light the candle, and enjoy an Italian meal in your new home." I told Joy that the person who captured Bill's heart was going to have the most thoughtful husband. I vowed to set them up, since they were both single.

Sitting on my driveway, looking out across the blue-sky-filled valley overlooking the town of Northfield, my heart was heavy. I was miserable in my job. I wanted to reduce my hours, but Art wanted us to work hard now so our retirement could be relaxed. We were always working or doing chores. The sun felt nice on my back. I was overwhelmed, thinking I was just tired and maybe a little depressed. We used our weekends to play catch up with chores, laundry, lawn, etc. On one of those weekend days we were getting ready for a storage shed to be delivered. The shed needed to have a flat, drainable surface to support the weight of the structure. A load of rocks was to be spread out so the people delivering on the following Monday could secure it on the bed of rocks. The pile loomed like a mountain and I knew I couldn't do it myself. Dave and Missy called and wanted to know if we wanted to go to Waitsfield to the falls for swimming. I said "No" because we needed to spread the pile of rocks. Art flipped out and threw one of our plastic Adirondacks style chairs over the deck because he really wanted to go. It was the first time I had ever seen his anger. It made me a little nervous, because I mentioned that it was his choice to have us do all the stuff on weekends because both of us worked during the week. I know it was a slam, but it was how I felt. As frugal as Art was with money, I took pride in keeping the house and property in tip-top shape. I wanted people to feel comfortable "dropping by," not feeling bad that the house was a mess. After all, my mom did keep a clean, welcoming home when she was alive. I related to her so much now.

It was July the following year and Jerry's mom wanted to come and visit. She wanted to see us ALL and spend time with us. She also requested to be able to see Jerry's remains. I had such mixed emotions, as I did when we discussed the funeral plans. Of course I agreed and looked forward to the visit. *How was I going to get this done?* Although I really WAS looking forward to their upcoming visit, I didn't want to tell her that my parents didn't want her anywhere near their place, as they remained somewhat bitter about the past. Plus, my thoughts triggered an unreasonable *conspiracy theory* that as soon as they knew where Jerry's remains were, they would go in the middle of the night and take Jerry's remains back to Ohio. I was so conflicted about what to do. I contemplated going up to my dad's and getting the cremated remains, bringing them down to my house, and putting them near a tree by our house. This would allow Jerry's mom to see them and avoid me even asking my parents. I mentioned the plans to Art when he came home.

"So what do you think?" I asked Art.

Art walked close to me and said "If you do that, then will you leave them here? What will Jerry III think? He will give it away knowing full well that his father's remains are up at Opa's house."

Now he came even closer and said, "Where is Jerry?"

"Haven't you been listening to what I just said?" I exclaimed.

"Where is Jerry really?" Art walked closer to me and stood directly in front of me. His six foot two eyes of blue lowered to mine. I had to look up into his. "I mean you are closest to Jerry in your heart. You carry your love for him and your memory for him every day in your heart. It's in the way you look at your son and in your everyday activity. It doesn't matter if they came up and took Jerry's remains and I think that it is crazy you would think that. The remains of his physical body are there, but he lives in you." With that he placed his very big hand on my chest closest to my heart, pulled me close to him and wiped the tears streaming from my face. *He was right.* I called my dad and told him the truth, saying that if they wanted to trek up into the pasture to what is intended to be a memorial then it should be allowed. No one was asking to go into the house or anything else. I was relieved when my father conceded.

You know, I can't even remember if we even went to Jerry's remains. We visited Stowe, touring the famous ice cream factory, went to Mt. Mansfield and its alpine slide, and then had a great lunch at one of the resort restaurants. It was a nice visit and it allowed Jerry's mom to get to know Art better as well as seeing her grandson. She even indicated she also considered Michael her grandson. That meant a lot to me. Art had adopted Jerry III and at least for the time being, I had not changed Jerry's name. I was not ready.

Art often shared with me his frustrations at working at Norwich.

"Sometimes they make no sense in admissions.... Do you know we don't send any recruiting material to any junior ROTCs in schools? It makes no sense," he would say. He was working hard to grow the corps and took his job very seriously.

I have said before that Art was passionate about Norwich and its deep traditions of honor and integrity. He shared the

Founder's Day concept of Alden Partridge who was the founder of Norwich. Alden Partridge went to nearby Dartmouth College, transferring to West Point, later becoming a superintendent. His ideas and concepts were too radical and he was asked to leave. He started the American Literary Scientific Academy, moving around New England when the Northfield townspeople gave land to Norwich. His radical ideals included living experiential learning labs and citizen soldiers. Art felt strongly that since the day was approaching we should have a Founders Day celebration for Norwich folks. Together with David and me, Art planned the celebration. We hosted a barbeque and during some comments he made he suggested that as faculty and staff those ideals and that history should be celebrated. Missy and Joy, along with Bill, faculty, and staff from around Norwich, attended the BBQ at our house, overlooking Norwich as well as my friends, Michael and Mini. Michael's wife, had just moved to Northfield, where Michael would work in the Army ROTC department of Norwich, instructing students in the Army corps of cadets lab held Tuesday afternoons. During the BBQ, I learned that Mike was a graduate of Norwich in the same class year as Bill. Mini (her real name was Donna, but everyone called her Mini) was pregnant and was due in the fall. I learned quickly talking with her that she was not happy to be in Vermont. I spoke to her about my move years ago and my mother's words about making the most of it. She had lots of energy around her and I felt instantly as though she was brought to Vermont for a purpose.

Art and I had been attending Grace Free Evangelical Church in town and both of us were working on marriage-building. Dave and Missy were our mentors and they often facilitated a group of us on weekday evenings. Childcare was provided. It was nice to share time with other adults outside of work and to grow in our personal relationships with Christ. We began to compromise and complete our household chores on Saturdays, leaving more opportunity to have Sunday for family and worship.

It was August and Dave and Missy called to see if we wanted to go on a hike. We had done our chores the day before, so it was easy to say yes. It was hot, but not too humid, like some August days in Vermont could be. The sky was bright blue. I packed some clothes in case we needed to change, as well as a picnic lunch. I suggested we go to "Mariawald" my Opa's camp in Waitsfield. It was only a short drive over a mountain and we parked at the end of a dirt road.

I fondly remembered when I was much younger and my Opa and mother were still alive. My family would pile into our VW van, which my mom and dad called "Nelliebelle," and go to camp. In those days somehow we would drive that VW right into camp on a road/trail leading to the Scragg Mountain trailhead. Now, either the state or the town had not maintained the road, which headed right over a gigantic boulder and wouldn't allow today's trucks to make it over. My family's property line did not come as far down the trail now and my dad traveled back and forth from Washington DC. Whenever my dad came up now, chores had to be done at home and "Mariawald" ended up being left unless time allowed. Things I remembered from growing up had become overgrown.

My parents had honeymooned at Mariawald, telling stories of sunbathing in the nude by a pond that through the years had dried up, since the stream bringing water from the top of the mountain and supplying fresh water to the pond had naturally moved away. My dad had attempted to bring back the pond when he had time, pointing out the rock on which my mother had laid out when the famous von Trapp grandchildren hiked there and startled the honeymoon couple. Those stories were fun to hear, as well as stories about when my Opa was alive and had held Mass in the chapel located on the camp property. I recalled the picture of the von Trapp's playing their instruments in the very crowded chapel.

As we walked/hiked, I pointed out the spots and recalled the stories I remembered. I pointed out where my friend Jean and I had come over the mountain on an adventure to pick out a Christmas tree, being so hungry, finding a can of creamed corn in our main cabin, and absolutely gobbling up what seemed like the best meal ever. I pointed out the overgrowing lot with barn, outhouse, chapel, and where the main cabin had been. A few years before, while I was living in Rhode Island, someone had set fire to the main cabin and we had not decided if we were going to rebuild. I showed Dave, Missy, the kids, and Art where as an infant and little child I would sit and a fountain that had been built by my great grandparents. A lily pond that stored water for the fountain and the main cabin was supplied by a line from the stream. A path led to the stream as well as to another "dunking spot" when it was hot. The barn had some bunk beds, a stove, and a now hide less deer bust in it, along with some wood and some tools. Nowadays the barn was left open for hunters or hikers. Before the main cabin had been burned, people would break into the barn frequently. They never stole the mower or the axe, although someone had stolen the antlers off the deer bust hanging on the wall.

Midsummer arrived and Art was very busy bringing in a large rook class. There are two different paths for students to go to Norwich, again steeped in the values of Alden Partridge, its founder. Some students choose to be traditional college students, while others choose the more disciplined military style of college, much like West Point, in its corps of cadets. A great difference was that at this university, those who went through the corps of cadets did not have to go into the military, unlike other military colleges. One of the other comments Art had shared with me was that he had overheard one of the admissions counselors on the phone with a prospective student say "of course you have to spend time in the military after graduation, which is why we a have a civilian side." I thought Art would explode as he reiterated the conversation. Since she had been there for a couple of years, he was convinced that she was one of the reasons the corps of cadets was not growing.

It was rook arrival day at Norwich. This was typically a very busy day as freshman corps of cadets students arrived at the school a week before the others to attend a basic training-like activity, preparing for life on the military side of Norwich University. Art had worked very hard in admissions to recruit what was looked at as the largest rook class in a decade. I was going to work and Missy was going to bring Jerry III down to meet me so he could go to the ear, nose, and throat (ENT) doctor to follow up on his many ear infections. I quickly visited my patients and went back to the office, where my boss Nancy wanted to talk to me. My job involved a full-time 36-40 hour week. She wanted to tell me that I could no longer just put in 36 hours, that even if my work was done in 36 hours I needed to stay for 40 hours a week. It had something to do with benefits. I was crying and very upset, because in my opinion, I was organized and knew my caseload enough to know how to see my patients. I never charged the agency for more than I worked. I asked if there was an option to decrease my hours and was told no.

Missy dropped off Jerry III and I shared with her my frustration. She left and little Jerry and I went to his appointment. Once it was over, still mulling over the sense of working 40 hours a week, I decided to take the scenic route home, traveling on Route 12 North instead of taking the interstate. The day was hot, but not too humid. I pulled in to Missy's driveway to pick up Michael. Missy came running out the door of her mudroom and had this very distraught look on her face. My immediate thought was something had happened to David, her husband. She started to take Jerry III out of the car in a hurried way and Maureen grabbed him and shuffled him into the house. I said, "Did something happen to David?"

Missy said, "No, it's Art. He has been rushed to the hospital."

"What happened?"

Art collapsed up at Jackman (Jackman Hall was the main administrative building on campus). "They think he had a heart attack," Missy exclaimed.

"Art had a heart attack? He was fine this morning. He said he just had a headache. The rooks were arriving today. He thought his headache was just stress," I said.

We went by the interstate to Central Vermont Hospital, where my mother had died twelve years ago. When we got to the red light just before the hospital, I had a very bad, sinking feeling that Art was dead. We parked and I was met by a doctor who led me into a room near where they were working on my husband. My dad was there. He had been in Vermont and Colonel D had called him and told him what had happened. The doctor who met me said the team was working on him. He started asking me questions. Had Art been ill, complained of anything. I mentioned the headache and wondered if Art had had an aneurism. That made more sense to me. Art was healthy. He worked out. He could eat anything he wanted to. It seemed like an eternity that we waited. The doctor came in and told me that Art had fought hard, that his heart had been stopping and starting, and that they couldn't seem to control it or keep it going, despite all of the equipment. He expressed his sorrow as they could not save him and left me in a dark, cold well of water. I was alone again.

I needed proof, once again. The doctor told me that I could take as much time as I wanted and described what I should expect.... The tubes that had been supplying Art with oxygen had been taken out. I remember asking for an autopsy to be sure. Art was 27, for heaven's sake. His body was kind of hard, cool to the touch. When I first saw Art, his eyes were opened. The whites of his eyes were bloodshot. *Petechial hemorrhage Heidi you know what that is. You have seen that in this very room when you worked here when you saw a couple of trauma victims come in from car accidents hangings and overdose*, which only made me feel like something had happened in his brain rather than his heart. I felt this even though, being a nurse, I knew that this often happened when the brain became depleted of oxygen. I remember holding his hand, his cold hand, and feeling cold myself; disbelieving this was happening to me. I cried until I couldn't cry anymore. The coldness just grabbed my own heart and broke over and over until a switch turned on. I had to make calls and once again plan a funeral. I asked the doctor if an autopsy could be done.

Arthur's time of death was 1:15 in the afternoon. The Reverend was at the hospital. Reverend Wick was the chaplain at Norwich. He gave me a hug and sat with me, praying with me. I remember feeling the comfort, but I also still carry that coldness and sheer angst in my body as if it happened a second ago.

Reverend Wick spoke at Art's funeral, giving a scriptural insight on the appropriateness of grief. He said that it is important for family, friends, and others to support those who have suffered loss, not just in the beginning when the death is fresh, but to continue for weeks, months, years. "Wait the weeks after the funeral and drop someone a line and let them know you are thinking of them." I had found this true with Jerry's death; however, I also found that people surround you and I have been very blessed to have such fabulous friends that outpour with love and support in times of tragedy. But eventually everyone goes on about their business and no matter how your heart is broken; the world doesn't stop for your grief. No matter how many friends you have, you will still feel lonely and lost at the times you need them most. I sought comfort in "being strong in the lord and his mighty power to heal" (Ephesians 6:10). I would get strong and choose to live, but it might take an eternity, for my heart was heavier and I felt the burden of picking up the pieces and moving on myself again. The Reverend also introduced the cadet prayer at Art's funeral.

Almighty God, in reverence for You, I seek to think and act in ways that are consistent with your perfect will. I humbly confess my failures and request forgiveness for my sins.

As a member of the corps of cadets, my desire is to reach beyond the mere requirements of our honor code and pursue an even higher standard of excellence – the one that You Yourself possess. Help me always to do what ethically is right. May I be the example – never the exception. May I be known for honesty in my words, fidelity to my commitments, and persistency in my responsibilities. May my effectiveness as a leader be measured by my strength of character, my trustworthiness, and others' willingness to follow me.

Lord God, may I always be above reproach, but never beyond scrutiny! Convict and correct me if ever my motives or methods lack integrity. And by Your grace, may I demonstrate the unbending courage to constantly reflect the best of what it means to be a Norwich Cadet. In Jesus' Name, Amen!

After listening to his insights and some hymns that Art loved: "A Mighty Fortress is our God" and "What a Friend we Have in Jesus," the Norwich Independent Battery honored one of its fallen with a twenty-one gun salute and echo taps. The commandant presented me with the folded American flag. In addition, following the service, Art's motorcade circled slowly around the upper parade ground where an artillery cannon and members of the corps of cadets stood in lines at attention paying their respects. The artillery cannon fired one last round, the sound of it echoing around the mountains surrounding the campus. Then all was silent. We all went home to start over again.

Missy and I would take long walks for exercise. During these times I would cry, laugh, reflect, and pray. "Missy, how can a woman widowed twice with two children ever find a great guy in the town of Northfield?" She often told me to have faith. The boys prayed each night with me … for strength, wisdom, healing… "and a daddy that will be there for me," Jerry III always added.

A grief counselor came to visit us. Her name was Ginny and she specialized in children's grief, but she explained that in order to help children, she needed to help the parents. She has written many books and was helpful to Jerry III and Michael. Jerry III seemed to have the most trouble. Ginny had him play with clay and face paint and assisted him in making a memory candle. We often talked about tragedy and loss. She had lost her brother and it inspired her to become a grief counselor – initially to give her something to do, but we had in common that it was to make it better for someone else so that they would never have to go through something the way we did without doing something productive. One of the things she explained to me was that with children, grief was essentially revisited through each stage of development the child went through. I recalled learning while in nursing school about the stages of grief. It wasn't comforting for me to know that suffering would continue for my children and for me.

During one of our walks Missy asked me, "If you could have one of your two husbands back, which one would, you choose?" After careful thought, I told her neither, because I loved them in very different ways and one of the things I was learning was that God had a real plan for me. I was living on a need to know basis and I wasn't allowed to see the big picture.

Art's death certificate came in the mail. The cause of death was sudden cardiac death (arrhythmia) due to myxomatous change of the mitral valve and fibromyxomatous thickening of the artery to the atrioventricular node. This was from a possible congenital defect. Because of Art's diagnosis and the fact that his dad had had heart disease, my next goal was to make sure that Michael didn't have the same issue. I discussed it with his pediatrician, who was more than happy to set up an appointment with cardiology, where I took Michael and had him checked out. Thankfully no issues were found, but every five years I would need to bring him back.

David and Missy were a godsend during this time. Jerry and I had gotten to know the couple while Jerry was in school at Norwich. David was an assistant commandant at the time and Jerry and I occasionally babysat their two girls, Emily and Sarah. Missy and I had really gotten to be close and she was godmother to both Jerry III and Michael, as well as babysitting for them while I worked. While Art was alive, David and Art became the best of friends. Art saw David as a spiritual mentor as well as a friend. His death hit David very hard.

It was very important now for me to have a will and establish guardians, as I had just had lightning strike twice. I established a will and appointed Missy and David as guardians of Jerry and Michael. Art thankfully had life insurance that he had bought from Jerry when he was alive, as well as insurance from the Marine Corps. What he didn't have was a will! It was unbelievable that even after all I had to go through with Jerry's death and probate in Ohio, I would face it again in Vermont. I asked the court to name David and Missy as guardians to the small amount of money from the Marine Corps that had to go to Jerry and Michael – even though I knew that the policy was supposed to go to his mother. No fighting the courts with minor children and without a will.

Another battle I had to fight was with the computer! When Art and I got married, I submitted my authority of doing all the bills to Art, who did everything on the computer. He hadn't shared the passwords with me. He had a handwritten notebook with figures, budgets, and other things. I contacted some of the day trading sites he used on the computer, as statements came in the mail and they were listed in his notebook. I could not seem to get the representatives to understand, even though they had all received death certificates that I needed to transfer the accounts to my name. They kept telling me that I wasn't the administrator of the account. *"Really?"* I thought. I'm pretty sure I know that. In the end, I won the battle, albeit not by the rules. Art's brother David, another tech-savvy guy, came up to visit and since he knew all of Art's personal information, he acted as though he were Art and got the passwords on the computer changed and voila! We were able to coordinate transferring everything Art was doing on the computer to a financial advisor. Then I took my place as head of household and would NEVER trust computers again with my financial information. Good old-fashioned checkbooks with registers for me.

Temperance

"Consider it pure joy, my brothers and sisters whenever

you face trials of many kinds, because you know

that the testing of your faith develops perseverance.

Perseverance must finish its work so that you

may be mature and complete, not lacking anything"

(James 1:2-4, NIV)

The garden Art planted was huge. I often sat on the rock overlooking our field, listening to the quiet. The air was warm, the sun beating on my back. I could hear the sounds of birds, leaves rustling in the ever-present breeze of our hill. Listening, crying, and thinking, I felt lonely, but comforted. I had a job to do ... complete the garden. It's amazing how big the garden was and how it flourished, not knowing all that had happened, not knowing its master was no longer there ... both weeds and plants, as the garden had not been tilled in weeks. The tomatoes of late August could be threatened by cold and as the days grew shorter, the snow loomed. The cordless phone rang. It was Colonel D. asking if he and Bill Passalacqua could drop by. Even though it was warm now in late August and the beginning of September, the temperature would drop and sometimes frost would come. The weeds were overwhelming and mentally I wasn't ready to take out Art's garden. Colonel D. and Bill came up. The colonel brought some cookies his wife had made and visited for a while. As it was getting dark, they offered to help cover the garden plants with the threat of the frost.

One thing was sure. I needed something to do. It was almost October. I wasn't ready to go back to work full time, as a visiting nurse. Missy would definitely watch the kids, but I wasn't ready to be away from them all the time. I spoke with my financial advisor, who was part of the board of the youth center in town. I had had this idea for a haunted hayride, since living in Ohio and going on one there. I told him that all over Ohio there were venues like this, where different groups would get involved to raise money for local causes. I had been to a couple while in Ohio. One in particular was very well run in the Springfield area. You felt as though you were driving to the middle of nowhere. Volunteers from the local eye bank parked cars for a $2.00 donation. You walked towards a house that looked vacant or at least darkened, to the side yard, where it looked like a lit-up carnival and where tickets were available. You hopped on a tractor-driven wagon with seats, after standing in line for an hour, building up anticipation to be scared. When Jerry had been alive, we took Jerry III to this. Kids stood in line, begging their parents to purchase glow necklaces, hot apple cider, or hot chocolate. Stepping on to the wagons, I had NO idea what to expect. As the wagon wound around the farm, different sites would come alive with themed events. One site was a dark sand-pitted area where heavy excavating equipment stood still. After a perfectly timed delay, the equipment came alive with crazily dressed clowns who crept toward the wagons. There were chainsaws and witches flying out from nowhere over your head, a crazy ambulance, a boat as we crossed a stream … screams and howls from people in the dark and just as many from the wagons. A fifteen- to twenty-minute ride was totally worth the $8.00 per person. The proceeds for this one haunt in particular went to the Jaycees. The boy scouts sold refreshments. "What a great concept. What do you think about it here in Vermont?" I asked John. "We could raise funds for the youth center." John told me it was huge, impossible, which made me want to do it even more. He looked at my enthusiasm and said, "All I wanted to do was interest you in being on the board of the youth center." Then he suggested that while I couldn't possibly pull it off this year, maybe I could contact some folks and get a haunted house going at the youth center and work towards next year, during Halloween. He mentioned I should talk to Sally D. and Frank from a group called Project Graduation. They ran a lot of fundraisers for a drug-and-substance-free graduation celebration for the high-school seniors. They were organizing the set up for a haunted house at the elementary school. While planning for the haunted house at the youth center, I went to theirs. I realized it would take their energy and knowledge to do a hayride and after seeing all the work that went in to decorating the elementary school, it could totally be done. I enlisted the help of Missy and Mini and went to Norwich to speak with Chan, who was the activity and intramural director. Frank, Sally, and my high-school friend Jeremy sat and listened to my vision as I described what could take place. They had a network of people and great skills of organization. Chan got the go-ahead to use some fields at Norwich and we planned on using rooks too to give them a chance to relax. My whole vision began as something to keep me busy and an opportunity to give back to the town for the attention and love provided for me during the death of my mother and the recent death of my husband. We would meet in January to begin planning for October.

I also planned a Halloween costume party at my house, again as a distraction. Normally I am not sure I would have had the energy to plan social events, but I decorated the house and dressed up. Joy came and I had invited Bill, Ed, Mike and Mini, Dave and Missy, Jean and David, and others. I did this at the same time I ran the haunted house, which did go quite well even though it was a lot of work. I was becoming an event planner.

I decided to have a New Year's Eve party. Again, diversions were important to keep me busy and help me. A lot of people came. I wasn't sure if they were coming because they knew I threw a good party or because they felt sorry for me. Well it didn't matter; it was keeping me entertained so it was working. I was upstairs looking down at the Christmas tree while talking to my sister and Jean. Elena commented that Bill seemed interested in me. I looked down towards him, we made eye contact, I smiled, and he returned the smile while he was talking to Mike and Mini. Jean agreed and also said, "Yeah, Ed appears like he's into you too." I shrugged and enjoyed the moment.... I kind of liked looking at Bill. Later that night Ed, Bill, Missy, and I were discussing movies and Ed asked the group if we had seen Titanic. I thought to myself that Art had really been excited for the movie to come out and that it was supposed to come out in August, but for some reason didn't get released to theatres until December.

Missy suggested that the next day, Bill, David, she, and I go to see it. And we all agreed. Missy said she would get the babysitter for the kids.

The movie was awesome. I enjoyed an outing without the kids and adult conversation on the way there. One of the thoughts I had during the movie occurred in a scene with Jack and Rose, the main characters. Jack had saved Rose from jumping overboard. Rose's demeaning fiancé, a rich 1st class passenger invites Jack to the captain's dining table to have a meal as a thank you for saving "his Rose." The table discusses Jack; sometimes as if he is not even there, interviewing him about what he does for a living. Jack explains that essentially he is a jack of all trades and that he has learned thus far that life is a gift and to make each day count. Rose lifts up her glass and makes a toast: "To making it count." I wondered if Art would have liked the movie as much as I did. I missed Art and it helped me to hear the words that Celine Dion sang: "My Heart Will Go On," by James Horner.

> "Every night in my dreams, I see you, I feel you; that is how I
> know you go on". …Forever this way, you are safe in my
> heart and my heart will go on and on."

It helps me to know that my heart will go on, that every love lasts for a lifetime. The heart remembers no matter where you are or where you're going. The song reminded me of when Art had touched me on my chest when Jerry's mom was coming for a visit and asked where Jerry was. It reminded me that each love is different and is stored forever, found deep within each of our hearts. I couldn't help but be reminded of A. L. Frink's *A Rose Beyond the Wall* and wondered if the character of Rose was based on it.

Progressively, under group watch, Bill and I saw each other. Bill came from a large Italian family in Geneva, New York. He was one of seven children, five of whom went to Norwich. Bill was older when he graduated, having obtained an associate degree in restaurant management at SUNY Cobleskill. He graduated in the class of 1988 and was the regimental commander or cadet colonel his senior year. David had also been the cadet colonel his senior year, had graduated two years prior, had gone in to the Air Force, and then came to Norwich as an assistant commandant. David was currently the alumni director at Norwich. Bill commissioned into the army after he graduated and after joined Norwich as an assistant commandant. That was how Art knew him. I learned that Bill had been a huge part in the solemn and humbling service for Art, the program, and encouraging the Reverend to add the cadet prayer to the service. Bill enjoyed cooking, family, and work. He had never been married and had no children. He told me that in high school he had dated Lauren Holly, although I had NO idea who she was, but Missy told me that she had been in several movies and a TV show, "Picket Fences." Apparently she had been married to Jim

Carrey and I laughed because I saw some resemblance between Bill and Jim Carrey.

Jerry's mom called to tell me a story she wanted to share. She hadn't always believed the strange things that happen to families in grief or at the time of death, but since her husband had died, some strange things had happened to her. "Laverne was Jerry Senior's oldest sister. She died young of alcoholism. She had a daughter MaryAnn. We haven't been in contact for many years, but she called me today to relay news that her dad had passed away from cancer that day. She told me that he was mostly comatose until recently (he had also remarried another woman named Laverne). Well, just before he died, he woke up and was talking to all his family in his second-floor hospital room. He waved towards the window and his wife said, 'I'm right here.' He said, 'I'm not waving at you; I'm waving at Jerry. He's come to take me to the Lord.' With that he closed his eyes and passed away." We had continued to keep in touch, sharing the grief and sorrow but growing independently. We seemed closer than ever, showing God's forgiveness from the past.

If Bill didn't see me with Dave or Missy, or coming over with either Colonel C. or Colonel D., I didn't see him or speak over the phone. Valentine's Day was coming. Missy invited the four of us to go to the August Lion, a very good restaurant in Randolph, about fourteen miles south of Northfield. The dinner was to happen on Valentine's Day. Bill said he would come and I looked forward to going out to eat. On the day we were supposed to go, Missy called and said that David was sick and they needed to cancel. I was crushed, as it appeared that Bill would only go somewhere with the others. I called him to break the news to him and suggested we go "together," without Dave or Missy. Bill hesitated slightly and agreed to carry on without our chaperones. He gave me a yellow rose and a card. At first it was awkward, especially since we saw several of Bill's students on dates and Bill appeared to stiffen up while introducing me. I kind of felt like maybe he was embarrassed and I briefly thought about one of the cadets saying something like "He'd better watch it with her because she is a black widow." I had been hearing people say things like that around town. We sat at a table in the middle of the dining room and there were a couple of times when I felt eyes on us, but also noticed that Bill appeared more comfortable. When we were finished, we drove back to my house and then Bill took the sitter home – and surprisingly came back to the house afterwards. I felt we progressed into a different phase in our relationship. Bill had at one time referred to phases. I never heard of that before.

I felt like we were going forward in our relationship. We had a nice weekend, spending quality time looking at ice sculptures, and went to my first wrestling match. Bill showed the boys and me a picture of his father and uncle when they played basketball at Norwich (they were both Hall of Fame players). Then we went back to his apartment for a tour and refreshments. I really like his taste. There was very brief couple time also, while I was trying to make sure Michael didn't get into anything, so it didn't last long, but I got a brief rub on the back. Then we went to my house for dinner. Dave and Missy were coming over since we still needed a little chaperoning. We had some time before dinner so all of us were just hanging in the living room. Bill sat next to me with his legs close to me. Jerry came down the stairs and called him Dad and then proceeded to ask him to be his new dad. I was horrified. No one made a big deal out of it. Bill told Jerry "Well your mom has all the prerequisites," as if Jerry knew what that meant. On this particular evening, Dave and Missy left and Bill stayed. We enjoyed getting to know each other and this time Bill even held my hand. That was a Saturday…. Then Sunday, Monday, Tuesday… nothing. I didn't even hear from him. I felt that there was a difference. I called and asked him to come up and Bill said he was busy. Wednesday he called and came over for coffee. He was reserved and sat on the opposite couch. I asked if there was anything wrong and he said no, but avoided my eyes. We even had trouble carrying on a conversation. I knew something must be up. I had no idea what was going on. I called Missy and told her this. She told me that the "old" Heidi would let it go, but that I needed to tell him how I felt. I asked her if she could come and do it, but she wouldn't. So on Thursday I asked him to come over for spaghetti. Now, keep in mind I am German, not Italian.

Anyway, he accepted. I was fine until about 5:30 p.m. Michael had gotten up that morning and thrown up and now I felt as though I would. So I started making dinner, just feeling all nerved up. He arrived for dinner and we began. I brought up the subject while cleaning up from dinner so I didn't have to meet his gaze. I had to excuse myself to go throw up. Wow! I was sick, not nervous. I agonized, but knew I needed to clear the air. I began by telling him that I felt as though we were doing really well and then felt like we just took five steps backwards. I laid it all out, that I thought of him in the morning, late at night, and that I was falling for him. He told me that on Saturday when he was over it suddenly dawned on him that as he was sitting in dining room with Michael on his lap that he was seeing himself married with two kids and there was so much he had missed. He referred to the movie, "She's Having a Baby." He needed to figure out what phase we were in. *There was that word again; what does that mean?* He asked me if I ever thought I would love again and I said that I was falling for him (after I went to bathroom and threw up again). I told him that he could ask me anything. At least I opened up. He went home, but at least I got a hug.

A couple of days later, I called him and with my nerves jangling in my stomach, I left a message on his machine just to say hi and see how his day went; wanting him to know without sounding too bold that I was thinking about him all day.... *Nothing like putting all the cards out there, huh?* Then he called back, which was even nicer, because that meant it was OK for me to say that. Even if he doesn't return my honesty, the hidden message is that at least it didn't scare him. I had just decided that with Art I was reserved and I didn't tell him a lot that I thought of him, how lucky I was to have him in my life, and just how important he was to me. I made that promise not to hold back, to try to get the most every day of everything.

For spring break, Missy and David and their kids, Jerry and Michael and I were driving to Florida. David and Missy and their family drove to Missy's mother's, but dropped us off on their way to Art's mother's to stay for the week. Art's mother lived very near my aunt, who lived in Merritt Island, and my grandmother, who towards the end of her life lived in the nursing home around the corner from Art's mother. Coincidently, my Aunt and "Nana," as the kids called her, were friends. I took the kids to Disney World and Nana came with us. Wow, it was very overwhelming, considering I had been at the age of 6 or 7, but to Disneyland in California. That was ages ago. The kids wanted to go everywhere and after a couple of hours there, my patience was fried and the kids were beginning to melt down. The next day, we visited the Brevard Zoo with my Aunt Marge and the kids became overwhelmed with that. I enjoyed it more than the kids.

During my visit, I would try to go for a run in the morning. The route I exercised on was a busy route with no sidewalks, going past an orange grove, new construction, and houses. A side road bypassed the main throughway around Merritt Island. It was also the route Art used to use to train when he came home on break from Norwich both he and Jerry Jr. had been on cross country team at Norwich at one point. It was Ash Wednesday. I started out my day, thinking things were different. It was almost too quiet. During my runs and walks on this road, I was always comforted by either a mourning dove or two, or cardinals. They would be sitting in the trees or along the wires along the road. This morning it was really quiet. In a slight panic, I ended up trying to look for the birds and fell and twisted my ankle. As I hobbled back to the house, I kept thinking of Bill. I thought about how I enjoyed talking with him; how I missed his dry humor, his smile, and his laugh. I couldn't believe that I was dreaming of him at night and thinking of him when I got up and when I went to bed. I would replay pieces of conversation we have had, tidbits of information, touches, feelings, laughing at funny things said or done. I memorized his face and the way he looked at me. It melted my heart. I found myself feeling intense. I prayed on my walk that day as I often did. Today's prayer was that Bill was in my future. I remember what a man by the name of Jose'N Harris once wrote, "To get something you never had, you have to do something you never did. When God takes something from your grasp, he is not punishing you but merely opening up your hands to receive something else. The will of

God will never take you where the grace of God will not protect you!"

Bill was great with the boys, who also prayed continuously for a new daddy. When I got back to the house, mom/Nana helped me ice my ankle. I was not going to let my ankle keep me from the beach, but knew I shouldn't drive, so Nana drove us the fifteen minutes to the beach. During this ride, and more during this visit, I was getting to know Art better, which both comforted and saddened me. I learned where he went to school, his friends, and a lot more about his feelings that he had expressed to his mother. Art's mom had been 42 when she had had Arthur. We talked a great bit about Art's dad and family. Art's mom was very easy to talk with. She and I discussed Bill and how I was beginning to feel for him and how God works in our lives. Bill and Art shared the same birthday! They were passionate about family and values and being Italian (although Art wasn't full Italian, because Nana said she was English), they also were both very passionate about Norwich. Nana, as I was learning, was placed in my life by a higher power to show the unconditional love Christ has for us. She missed Arthur terribly, but knew that my life needed to move forward, as she often mentioned.

I spoke with Bill while we were there. He seemed distant and reserved again. He was headed to Germany with the Regimental Band. *I am tired of playing that game.* In a burst of strength and German stubbornness, I felt *I know he has a lot of thoughts, but I can do this on my own if he doesn't feel the same.* It is so confusing having to be patient. I prayed for patience and now was convinced that God was placing Bill in my path because I was impatient and Bill was the perfect lesson in patience. My whole life up to now has had the mentality of "hurry up and wait." I couldn't control this situation, just like the deaths and the ongoing grief I was feeling. How would my faith get me through trying to figure this man out?

   We made excellent time driving back, with Missy and I driving because Dave's back was out. Bill came over and brought me flowers. I thought *I am so confused by this man and so intensely interested.* He stayed for a little bit and helped me put the kids to bed. He came downstairs and his face was beet red. I asked him what was up and he told me that when he put Jerry III to bed, Jerry III told him that he needed to kiss his mom, on the lips and needed to "linger." I had NO idea where he got that from, but now I was beet red. Yet, Bill didn't kiss me on the cheek as he had done on previous occasions, but put his hand to my neck, leaning as if he would kiss me on the cheek and then kissed me square on the lips and "lingered"!!! When I closed the door I was so energized, I wanted to jump up and down. I was electrified and invigorated! In my journal I wrote Subject: The kiss. The focus or symbol of a relationship changing from casual to something a little more. What makes it? I mean it (the kiss) has been around. You kiss as a greeting, whether it be on the lips or cheek, you kiss hello; you kiss goodbye or for New Year's, but when you share one with someone you're attracted to it means so much. Energy passes: when the kiss is on the cheek, you're like "okay," but when it's on the lips you're like OKAY, NOW THAT'S SOMETHING. Then you want to do cartwheels, jump up and down, or run around the building a dozen times. My son one night (age 4½) gave these lessons to Bill. I mean, as if he knows what that word even means. That's what it is though, not a quick peck because that's just sparks but a "linger"; now that is fireworks! I held on to that moment for the next fourteen days while Bill travelled to Germany.

Bill came back from Germany and called me to say he was back safely. He said he was going in to work and I would talk to or see him later. Well, I saw him working out at the gym while Missy and I were running. I invited him up for dinner and he said "we will communicate." *Doesn't that just mean "NO" in man talk?* I mean really I would think he could just tell me if he doesn't plan on seeing me. So, I was definitely hurt when all I got was a phone call and Colonel C. got a visit. Fourteen days away from him and he goes to see the Colonel. The kiss would have to last longer for me. Patience, Lord God....

After being abrupt with him, I called him back and told him how I felt. He said he was sorry and missed me too. It was 100% obvious that my heart was leading the way with me, while my head was in the cosmos. It was hard not thinking of him and what he was doing and wondering whether I will be in his life. I felt such loss of control and wanted to be with him all the time. The hardest part was thinking he didn't feel the same way.

Bill spent time every once in a while with a group of Italian men in the area. They were older gentlemen that were in the neighborhood. They would all cook a meal and share fellowship. Bill mentioned before we started "dating" that on Saturday mornings they would often meet at the town barbershop for coffee. Francesco, the owner, had come straight from Italy had a very sharp accent often claimed he would give "the besta haircut inawh town!" Bill would go down for and meet up with the guys- Gene, Col. C, Tony, and Mr. Politi. They would sometimes have dinner where they would cook at each other's houses making authentic Italian meals. Francesco often came up to my house and cooked meals that you would think there were thirty people coming for dinner and it was just Bill, Jerry and I, or Col. C joining us.

Jerry III birthday arrived. Such joy for my son as he turned five; always overshadowed by the fact that his dad died the very next day EVERY YEAR. I tried to be joyous. I just wanted to be held and told everything would be okay. I wanted Bill to be the one to hold me. Instead, he wanted "Bill" time. My expectations weren't being met. To top it all off, the snow came down off of our roof. The way our house was built, the steep pitch of the roof came over the garage. I married a genius, who along with a genius contractor did not figure out that any large amount of snow would eventually fall right in front of the garage. The garage fit two-vehicles and it was controlled by an industrial-sized door. We had gotten several inches of snow the night before that emptied when the roof heated up. It was a great roof, but it left a glacier of snow packed like an avalanche four feet deep, two car lengths long, and six feet across. Everyone was busy and I looked at the snow and thought – *naturally!* Love is patient... love is Kind.... I can't say I felt love of any kind, even for God looking at that pile. Then I started laughing at myself. OK, now I am going daffy. The voice inside my head talked back and said ... turn your frustration into something productive and I thought of a verse by Patrice Gifford: "It is always wise to stop wishing for things long enough to enjoy the fragrance of those now flowering." It took me hours to shovel.... I was exhausted and triumphant and the burden was lifted from me. God showed me I could do this myself with my own physical and mental strength. I didn't feel sorry for myself. I was directed. I was determined.... I was not only going to get through my grief and whatever entered my path, but as soon as I could I was going to get a snow blower!

Bill came over and we had a very nice quiet evening with some good conversation. Bill shared with me that he felt we skipped the "phases" and he wasn't comfortable moving ahead without them. He won't even admit we are dating to people or that he has a girlfriend. That bothers me. I told Bill I was patient, but that I felt out of control. I did not tell him that I loved him. He asked me "what is love?" So after he left I stayed up until 1:30 a.m. writing what I thought about love. It occurred to me that even though Bill has never told anyone that he loved me, he was acting as though he was a man in love. I knew how I felt, but I wasn't going to tell him. I had been in love before, after all. I did come to the conclusion that when Bill told someone he was in love with them… he would mean it. He was older than me, but I was more experienced. Was this a glimmer of patience? Was I OK with this?

I got a call a few days later. It was Bill and his voice sounded very strained. His father had passed away. He was on his way back to his hometown. He asked me to take his key and look after his place, since he didn't know how long he would be gone. When he told me, it brought back feelings of anguish. I just wanted to hold him and protect him and cry. Bill had lost his mother the same year as mine. She had died of complications of pneumonia. His dad had been in a restaurant and had died of what they thought was a heart attack; although he had had an angioplasty recently and a history of diabetes. Francesco, Colonel C., Colonel D., David, Missy, the other assistant commandants Bill worked with – Steve, Mike, Helen, and some cadets plus the Reverend – rented a van and we headed to New York for the funeral. Bill's father had been a Hall of Fame football player and basketball player at Norwich. Some folks at Norwich often spoke about Bill's father and uncle, saying that there might not have been a football program at Norwich had it not been for the two men, as they had come to Norwich from Hartwick college and Hartwick's program had ended so Norwich had hired the coach, Duke, and he brought Bill's family with him. Other Norwich folks also attended. We all wanted to show our support for a good man. I left the boys with Jack and Jodi. It was in "G" town, or Geneva, that I was able to meet his family and gain an understanding of Bill. His family called Bill "Billy," as did Colonel C. I was flattered when Bill's two sisters, Terri and Mona, and his sister-in-law Kathleen stood around while I had offered to do some dishes after the funeral and they mentioned that they had heard of me and were happy to meet me, even though it was under these circumstances. Bill was the sixth child and you could tell they were all so proud of "Billy." I apparently passed some sort of test, because when I returned, I heard from him every day while he was gone.

He came up and surprised me at home. I was not expecting him, as in the past he usually called or I just wouldn't see him. Jerry III said "we really missed you, ya know!" Bill grabbed my hands and pulled me up to him and gave me a big hug and kiss, all while Jerry III was saying "can you be my daddy…" I told Jerry III not to worry about it and Bill said "Jerry, you just never know these days." I felt closer to him. Since he had left his key, he came up to get it, so he did not get to read the letter I left for him at his place. It seemed our thoughts crossed in the air. I essentially told him in the letter that I was sorry about his dad, that I love him as my friend, and more. He called me when he read it to tell me that it brought tears to his eyes.

In May, Bill traveled with Jerry III, Michael, and me to Ohio to see Jerry Jr.'s family. Emily was graduating from the University of Dayton and Philip would be graduating from high school in the near future. We stayed at my friend Joy's house. Jerry's mom and Nanny really seemed to get along with Bill. To some degree, it was a test on my part, because I really wanted my relatives to get to know Bill and to know, again, how much it meant to me to have a relationship with Jerry's and Art's families. I would not make another mistake by not involving my love-related family. Whatever they chose to do with the information I presented them would be their choice and I could not control it. *Progress for me*, I thought. During the visit, we went to Gama's house. She had moved from the townhouse when Jerry and his dad were alive to a house that she had lived in earlier in her marriage. The house was one of the many that Bampa had built, with a pool out back. It was made of brick, colonial style. We went in and all of us congregated out in the back where the pool was and the sun was shining. Patrick changed and went in the pool without being prodded. Jerry III also went in and I had to laugh to myself, because after Jerry Jr had died, Patrick had nearly scared the bejesus out of Jerry III by jumping in the pool with him and Jerry III had been afraid of swimming for the entire summer while I lived in Ohio. He would wade in after that, but certainly not swim. Now, he went right in by himself. Michael now a two year old was also a swimmer, but did not like to get his head wet at this point and couldn't swim by himself, even though I had been taking him for lessons at the pool. After some time of swimming, we opened presents and enjoyed the patio outside, while Patrick took Nanny back to her house. I was very comfortable with Bill making conversation with Nanny, noting that he spoke very easily with everyone. Michael had started walking around the pool edging closer and closer. I was just about to open my mouth to tell him to get away from the edge… or… he would fall in, when he did just that. Emily was at the pool edge in a flash and grabbed him right out. All I could remember was his wide open eyes sinking in that water. That set the tone for Michael and *finally* he listened. He hung closer to his Aunt Emily after that.

Bill and Art shared the same birthday, June 2. At one point in the conversation, Bill had indicated that because he had come from such a large family his birthday was never a big celebration. I decided we would change that and set about planning a surprise birthday for him. I asked him out for his birthday. I told him I would take him for a surprise to Burlington – hinting about taking him on a dinner cruise on Lake Champlain and making sure he brought a jacket for possible cool, wet weather. I arranged to have all the guests in the big garage of my house, even having them picked up at Norwich and brought to the house to avoid making Bill suspicious. The door was closed and Jerry III looked out, down the hill at the tree line to see when his car was coming. When Bill pulled into the driveway, up to the garage, and got out, moving toward the side door, I opened it and everyone yelled "surprise!" I snapped a picture of him in total surprise with the 70 or so people that made it to his party.

On my birthday, a couple of weeks after Bill's, he presented me with a series of presents. One was a new journal. In it, he wrote, "I thought it would be nice if we had a book to record the moments that we share, full of firsts. Its pages would offer us a future look at special memories as a pair. The contents might list a trip or a rock-n-roll band. As long as were together, walking hand in hand." I had already been recording all of my thoughts and firsts as a way to process all I was going through.

Another present was a set of ear protectors for the riding lawn mower with a note… "So you never miss the words… I LOVE YOU! - Bill." This day was the best gift of all, hearing those words and knowing that he hadn't said it to anyone else, except his family. He showed me that day that you can't make someone love you; all you can do is be someone who can be loved. The rest is up to him. From that day, Bill told me every day that he loved me. We entered into another phase I had never experienced in this manner. Amidst my pain and sorrow, I found such joy in knowing that Bill loved me, which also meant he loved Jerry III and Michael.

We spent the rest of the summer continuing to get to know each other; we added to the journal of firsts going to Maine as a family, with our chaperones Dave and Missy of course and their kids and my sister and her two girls. Maine was a special place for me. Jerry and I had trekked to Ogunquit, Maine and visited Walkers Point, one of the homes of the Bush family, while we were on our honeymoon. In particular, Ogunquit beach changed pretty much every day and was one of the cleanest beaches I have ever been to since both the tide and the river, which formed a delta there, washed the area. It was ice cold, bone chilling cold, even at the height of summer. The ocean was renewing for me and it was renewing to share it with people close to me. The sound of the waves rolling and crashing with the surf snapping made peace with me. There was a walking path called the Marginal Way that people could walk from Ogunquit to Perkins Pier. The walks or "runs" in the mornings were nice as the sounds of the ocean and birds were so peaceful. You could distantly hear the sounds of boats whirring by at times in between the waves crashing. Art and I vacationed in Ogunquit while he was alive. We returned to the same place. I had never been to stay "in" such a nice place, as we had only camped when I was younger where overlooking the ocean, in the middle of the resort, was a fenced-in area with children's pool, adult pool, hot tub, and bar. Wait staff would walk around and it was nice to be able to order a cold drink and put it on your room tab. I remembered respectfully all the planning my mother had done to go camping.... It was an enormous task, but essential for our family then, as it was the only way my dad could break away from his command. No contact unless the state police tracked him down. The ocean resort was nice, watching fireworks over the water, building sand castles, and walks along the shore.

Later that summer, we went white-water rafting in Lake George, New York for the day, just the two of us. It was a freshman send-off for the university, so it was like a business trip. David and Missy stayed behind and watched the boys.

The beginning of August brought another Founder's Day at Norwich. Since Art had planned the inaugural event, bringing attention to the date, Bill and David felt this tradition should continue. They approached the president of the university to have it at Norwich and David planned it from the Alumni office. Now it was at the school under Alden Partridge's statue. Bill, during this time, had transitioned from the commandant's office and briefly worked in admissions until an opening as assistant director of alumni affairs became available and then Bill moved in to that position.

Mid-August brought another rook arrival day, which meant another dreaded anniversary. The grief counselor had encouraged me to do something to mark the day and with David, Missy, Bill, and others we marked the day by bringing flowers to the Harmon Wall, where both Art and Jerry's names were now engraved among the rest of the fallen alums. The day was sullen and we tried to keep busy. The day before, Norwich had had another sudden cardiac death. A math professor had been playing racquetball and collapsed and died. I just couldn't stand by and watch this happen again.

I contacted the president at Norwich and made an appointment to speak with him. My goal was to tell him that perhaps if Art had had an AED (Automated External Defibrillator) in the early onset of his symptoms, he might have survived. Now that the math professor had died, it became clear to me that I needed to ensure that no other family endure such grief. I researched and presented the idea to the president and he presented to the board of trustees. Charlie H., one of the trustees, thought it was an absolutely brilliant idea and they approved placing defibrillators in security vehicles, since security staff were often the first responders. That would also pave the way to have the AEDs in the athletics buildings. I then assisted in getting a rural development grant to assist the local first responders in doing the same.

October brought about our haunted hayride. This promised to be busy and it was a huge success. There were logistical problems with weather and the cold, but it was a new and exciting event that drew the attention of the local news, which did a live broadcast. Two hundred or more volunteers participated. The small crew of organizers got the nickname of "skeleton crew." I was given the title of general. We raised several thousand dollars the first year. As a committee, we had decided the proceeds would be divided and given to three youth-related groups: a group called Project Graduation, the local youth center, and a community service scholarship for a Norwich student. The volunteers loved it – even though they endured cold, windy weather. A new tradition in Northfield was established. Another first for my journal.

It was a beautiful December evening. Bill invited me to Burlington for dinner. I had heard some intelligence and felt in my heart that Bill would ask me to marry him. I was content knowing that the question would come, but anxious about when. I had learned over the last year or so that patience was needed. We went to a restaurant called the Cork and Board. It was a German restaurant. I had the Jaeger schnitzel and Bill had the sauerbraten. I thought many times during dinner – *this could be the time*... then nothing. The tiny white lights that lit the inside of the restaurant were so romantic, the music, enchanting. We went to Church Street, which sits up on a hill overlooking Lake Champlain, where there were more white lights and there was more romance. We got coffee and dessert and walked around. Lots of people filtered around, doing their holiday shopping.

There were Christmas carols. *Still nothing.* We drove home and I
needed not to be angry or disappointed. We drove "the back way
home" which was from the Capital of Vermont, in Montpelier,
south instead of taking the interstate. Bill suggested we go for a
walk around the Norwich Campus. We walked around the upper
parade ground, usually busy with students going to class,
marching, parades, snow sculptures, or snowball fights. Exams
were winding down now and it was quiet. We saw a few students
who had last minute exams walking about. We walked over to a
staircase that NO freshman was allowed to go up or down, called
Centennial Stairs. The stairs were made of granite and engraved
with distinguished alumni or people who had contributed to the
ideals and values of Norwich. I thought about that and then
looked on the mountain before me. It had been the ski area at one
time, where I had first learned to ski as well, like so many
students at Norwich. It had been dismantled just a few years
before, since there was no snow-making equipment and there
were liability issues, it made it harder for Norwich to run it as a
ski slope. Now students or community members would go
sliding. I watched as tonight two snowmobiles were coming
down the face of the steep mountain. I turned to my left and saw
Bill's face. The look was very serious. My stomach lurched. He
kissed me and the kiss was so serious and so intense that I started
shaking (although it could have also been the cold). He pulled
out a very nicely decorated gift bag from his pocket. Bill got

down on his knee and said, "Heidi, I love you. Will you, Jerry and Michael spend the rest of your lives with me?" Bill had tears in his eyes and I was also tearing up. I said yes and kissed him. We went home to share the news. I was so excited for the kids, looking forward to their reactions. Jerry III rolled his eyes when we told him and Michael hugged Bill. The love I felt for Bill was so strong it stirred my soul. I wrote in my journal that night, reflecting on the evening. On one of the nights that Bill had asked me what love is, I wrote down so many things. I asked my heart, why is love effective? A song can stir feelings, but love stirs the soul. What is love? LOVE is the most powerful force in nature, the universe, from human form to the love of God. I know I love him because of all the things he does. I love the way he laughs. I love the way he will say something and then ask me, "what do you think about that?" I love how he cooks and how thoughtful he is about making sure everyone is taken care of. I love how he handles the boys. I love how he doesn't like the kids to come to the table without a shirt on. I love how good he is with them, reading to them, playing with them, and how he calls the boys children instead of "kids." I love and respect him tremendously. To want love will block the way you must love all. You must love or you cannot dwell in the house of the lord. Jesus says if you practice love he will bless you exceedingly above all. Leave it all to him. Peace will come and trust. (1 John 4:16)

This I swear is my final wedding to plan. Please, dear God, may it be my last wedding unless I have so many more children or I take up wedding planning as a side job. We set the date for May 1, a spring wedding. I asked Missy to be my matron of honor. My friends Jean, Sonia, and Sara, as well as Kellie, who had endured all of my loss with me, would be in the wedding, as would Mini. Bill asked Colonel C. to be his best man and Jerry III and Michael would be mini best men. Jerry III would carry the rings. He also asked his brothers Sam, Gary, Steve, Ron, and his brother-in-law Randy to be groomsmen. Bill's sister Mona would do readings. My "brother" Gary's daughter Erin would be the flower girl. Bill and I felt that since Norwich was so engrained in our relationship, we should get married at the white chapel on campus. Art and I had been married there and even though his funeral had also been there, this was the right place. Bill and I were Catholic and I asked Father Lavalley and Father Deforge to perform the mass. Neither were available, so they encouraged me to ask the priest in town. I asked him, but because he felt we should be having our service at *his* parish in town (and where Jerry and I had married), he declined. We were disappointed, but it was short lived, as God had a different plan. Reverend Wick was available and felt honored to be a part (secretly all along I had hoped he would be the one available). In addition, I felt it important to have Jerry and Art's moms involved in the ceremony. This time I knew that it not only felt like the right thing to do, but it was important to me to have them involved. It was important for me to show them I wanted them in our lives.

We would combine the traditions of Italians and Germans and opted for a renaissance theme – not to the extreme with armor and jousting, but we included a meal and an arbor with lemons, ivy, oranges, and grapes. We would also give all our out-of-town guests gift bags with a taste of Vermont. Bill created a note of welcome on scroll paper, along with things for out-of-town guests to do. We placed items like summer sausage, cheddar cheese, bottled water, biscotti, and chocolate, all made in Vermont.

I was walking along a road. There was a bit of snow covering the hillside to my right as the hill was elevated and on the other side of the road, the same snow sloped downward to a depth I didn't know. Dark black clouds loomed above my head. I followed the road, walking to a destination unknown. In front of me, I spied a beautiful post-and-beam constructed house, a green roof similar to my own home. There was an inviting porch that appeared to wrap around the entire structure. There were no cars in the yard and the door was wide open. I looked behind me. No one was behind me and the clouds were dark and uninviting, while what was before me I didn't know. I made the choice to walk in. It was brightly lit, despite the lack of light and the clouds on the path I had just come. In fact, I had been thinking that the clouds were ominous behind me with this beautiful place inviting me in. The place was very comfortable, familiar even; cast in a lodge-like décor – green and maroon plaid furniture in what looked like a living room with a fire in the fireplace. "Hello?" The sound of my open-ended greeting echoed somewhat throughout the house.

I thought I heard a response further back in the house. I walked cautiously, yet felt very comfortable in this place, as though I had been here before. It really felt quite spa-like. There was the sound of a waterfall inside the house and if I listened a little more, even rhythmic wavelike sounds. I continued down the hallway, which seemed to go endlessly, until I came to a desk. Behind tit sat Colonel D. He spoke, a smile on his face, but was very serious and gruff. It did not make me feel uncomfortable, which was weird, as that was how I knew Colonel D. to be. He told me that my life was changing and my gloom was behind me. He motioned to the door behind him to his right and told me to choose the door, slightly ajar but unrevealing of its meaning. Very calmly and peacefully, I heeded his instruction. I opened the door and peered curiously through it. I walked through the door onto a small porch. In front of me was the most beautiful meadow of green grass, bright and sunny, with flowers scattered around me. I tried to avoid them, which somehow I was doing quite perfectly. There were three of the brightest and purest white lambs walking about along the hillside, grazing under the warmest sun to my right. Looking up onto the hillside, I had to do *a double-take, as a child of just toddler age – who didn't look much more than a year old – came down the slope walking amongst the lambs with brownish-blonde hair in long wisps along the nape of its neck. The child was a little girl (I felt), and had the bluest, most perfect eyes so that when the little child smiled, she had the most perfect glow about her. The cast of her hair from the sun made me feel so incredibly comfortable and at peace. No one spoke to me except for Colonel D., but I somehow knew that my life had reached an entirely new level. I woke up feeling an incredible sense of happiness, as if a cloud had been lifted from me. I was going to be fine.*

Wisdom

"Having knowledge through years
of learning and experience"
Get wisdom! Get Understanding
Proverbs 4:5

In May it was actually dry and humid. The snow had finally melted on our hill. The bridal party went to get our hair done and makeup. Jerry III and Michael, dressed in little black tuxedos and looked sharp. I was nervous to see if they would handle all the commotion of the wedding. Jerry III was so excited to ride in a limousine. It was a first time for me, as it was for him. Michael had a look about him. It was like he was going to resist walking down the aisle with his brother. My dad and mom had already made a plan to snag him if he became an issue.

Jerry's mom and his brother Philip came to the wedding from Ohio, along with some of Art's family from New Jersey. I asked Jerry's mom to light the unity candle along with Bill's Aunt Phil during the ceremony.

My dress was ivory, with a scoop neck. There was no train to the dress as I had had from my first wedding. The dress was beaded with the same style as the bridesmaids around the neck and mine was also beaded around the sleeves. The bridal party dresses were ruby red in color, somewhat velvet feeling. The flowers also had a Renaissance theme. They didn't have just flowers in them, there were grapes and ivy also included. As each of the female guests entered the chapel, Francesco handed each a rose. My friend Kellie handed out the program. The Reverend, who I have seen officiate one wedding and a funeral, just took my breath away with his words. If I hadn't been singing, I would have been crying.

The ceremony was magical, spiritual. Hilary, a former student of both Art and Bill, accompanied me on the piano to sing to my new husband. The words, from Shania Twain, could not have been more appropriate. Spoken, I started…

"I do swear … that I'll always be there. I'd give anything and everything, and I will always care. In weakness and strength, happiness and sorrow, I will love you… with every beat of my heart." Then with all the joy in my heart I sang the song From This Moment On, with all the emotion I could without crying. Most everyone else did..

Bill's Brother Ron sang and played the piano. David did a reading and spoke to the witnesses gathered. Sonia also spoke.

The reception was equally nice, seeing and sharing the day with over two hundred people at the Capital Plaza Hotel in Montpelier. The owner is a Norwich graduate. One of their rooms was a huge ballroom. Pretty much all our out-of-town guests stayed there, including Bill and me on our wedding night. We decided on a several course meal in addition to cocktail hour to go along with our theme. Missy's sister-in-law Maria contributed; being an Italian woman, she had a recipe for Italian wedding soup (for which I believe to this day they still use the recipe). Guests had their choice of lamb, chicken, or fish. There was an open bar and we served a German wine called Gewürztraminer. We chose the cake to go with the Italian theme, but also had Italian cookies and desserts planned. This was the first time I was not rushing. God willing, it would be the last wedding of my own. The wedding party, as well as guests, arrived and walked through an arbor of grapes, ivy, oranges, and lemons designed by our local greenhouse and the florist, again with our Italian theme in mind. Each table had cameras, so people could capture photos of moments that Bill and I might enjoy later. We also decided to have a time capsule. On each of the tables was a letter and we asked each table to write something on that on specific dates, first anniversary, second, third, fifth, tenth, etc., we would have certain guesstimates of where we might be – how many kids, where we might be living, goals attained, etc. My one desire sweet Jesus Lord was for a long, happy, healthy life with Bill. We had a DJ and danced and celebrated into the night. Michael fell asleep in one of the corners of the room. Earlier he had had an accident in his tuxedo pants and my parents had quickly gone home to have him change. He would only change into the holiest of jeans and boots. He kept his tuxedo, shirt, tie, and jacket on, however, and came to the reception in style.

I learned that evening that Bill is an Elvis Presley enthusiast. He did an impression of one of his songs with dance moves I had never imagined Bill would do. He never ceases to amaze or surprise me.

Bill and I woke very early the next morning (I believe we saw Bill's brothers were still up) to drive two hours south to ride an airplane to Florida, where we would board a cruise ship and sail to Tortola, Puerto Rico, and St. Thomas for seven days. It was amazing to see sights, soak up sun, and shop while each night we were able to fine dine and honeymoon.

Returning from the cruise, we drove up to Art's mother's house and stayed a couple of days, taking in the sites of Cape Canaveral and visiting, finally returning home where we settled in to a quiet yet busy household with complete peace.

January 18, we welcomed the most beautiful little baby girl, a most precious gift. My labor was all centered on God. The staff commented that it was a very peaceful birth. She had sandy blonde hair and the most beautiful blue eyes. I flashed back to my dream prior to being married of that little toddler blonde on the hillside and felt pure joy. Bill and I had talked about naming our baby girl Angelina, but settled on Julia, quite coincidently finding out that after Bill's father made a great golf putt or play on the golf course he would remark "JULIA!" youthful, joyous. Bill's dad put the name right into our minds.

"For the wisdom of this world is foolishness to God" (1 Corinthians 3:19). During my life I have reflected on how little any one person knows and how limited one person's wisdom is. Each of us has some insight, knowledge, and wisdom that we learn throughout our lives, but the scope of it is usually fairly narrow and limited to our sphere of influence and knowledge of our world. What we experience and how we experience develops into wisdom. I've gained knowledge for sure, experience, for sure. Some translations of the Bible say "the fear of the Lord is the beginning of knowledge" (Proverbs 1:7). It finally came to me. When I finally started to recognize that all this experience was about my relationship with people AND about God, that was the beginning of wisdom. That gave me the right to tell others what I've learned and that makes me wiser.

Here is some of the wisdom I have learned to pass on. If you had only a short time to live – an hour or two, what would you do? I'll give you this advice, if you'll take it. Don't take it for granted that you will have that person there. Say that you love them. Say that you care. Do those things that you have put off because you think you don't have time. Don't wait. Do them!

My kids when they were little would tell me the entire time "luv ya mommy," or "I love you to finity (infinity) and beyond." They progressed to saying "good night" and saying "love you mom," and then hardly saying it unless someone spoke first (good grief: if they could only do that for other things. Tee hee).

To some this may sound cold. To some you may understand. In grief, EVERYONE is different. Every situation is different. The stages, although "defined" by many very important scholarly types, are different. No two deaths are the same, as no two individuals are the same. No two loves are the same. So, unless you are living that reality each day or minute, trying to cope with death, don't let it rule you – you rule it. Don't live as if you're that individual; don't tell others what to do. **There are no rules**. **There is no set time** in the grief process that determines when a person can get on with living, **but there is a choice:** Do it and you will be free; don't and it will be a living hell. **I choose to live**. I choose to make my life and the life God has given me count.

I have asked myself this several times throughout the last 40 plus years since my mom died. Part of the wisdom I have to share is that we have all experienced this grief in some form it's just I have unfortunately experienced in a compact short way and in major loss of death. Some experience it in disappointment, in the end of a relationship, loss of a job, loss of limb, paralysis, etc. What is grief? What is "normal grief" vs. unresolved grief or what is now being called complicated grief? I should tell you that I cannot tell you what is "normal" only what clinicians will tell you is "normal". Clinicians will tell you that it is more about behavior or emotions when they talk about grief. Grief is an emotional response that is a complex, broad spectrum and by no means subject to no judgment by anyone. Clinicians note that over time in the absence of "complications" grief progresses. As I've learned and experienced my pain and grief was overwhelming, but that adage "time heals all wounds," does work. Not a day goes by that I don't think of my mom, or Jerry, or my father in law, Art, or friends I've lost, but the wound is less deep, it burns less, I suffer less. I think of them in reverence. In comparison, when the symptoms linger, or when one cannot think of a loved one or they obsess over them beyond the first few months some clinician's refer to this now as "complicated grief". It has similar features as major depression and post-traumatic stress disorder (PTSD). If you are not able to move forward there is help and I encourage you to share your burdens. Make your feelings count, whatever they are. Here's to making "it" count.

Postlude

As I have sat here and put words to paper, mostly concerning the last two decades or so of my experience, I just wanted to give you an additional thought. I began almost every year since Art died saying that I would write a book. I was always unavailable to do it.... Too busy, want to be outside; I have to do this, got to do that. It wasn't the right moment. I thought I could do a little at a time. In January 2010, 25 years after the death of my mother and the start of these experiences, I almost died. I was diagnosed with a perforated colon and my doctor performed life-saving procedures. As a result I have a temporary colostomy and an open wound. Things look promising for me to have my colostomy taken down and I can return to the activities I did when life presented me with some more choices. I could choose to live or I could be the victim. I chose to take the opportunity God presented to me, because now I had no excuse to avoid using the time in my mind and spirit life to share the journey with you. I had to get through the feelings of being the EXACT same age my mother was when she died and EXACTLY the same time of year, with a child that was EXACTLY the same age as I was when my mother died. I am thankful for the opportunity and I hope you can have the courage, temperance, honor, and wisdom that God gives to you to make the choice to make it count. Give it a try!

From My Journal: Thoughts as They Came

What makes some people handle the stress of crisis with strength and hope and others crawl into bed and wish it away? FAITH is the answer.

Healing occurs as you admit to yourself that a power higher than you is in control and there isn't a darn thing you can do – so you go on because you CAN control that!

"When the soul is full of peace and joy, outward surroundings and circumstances are of comparatively little account" (Hannah Smith).

I've learned it is not <u>what</u> you have in your life, but <u>WHO</u> you have in your life that counts.

You feel perfectly giddy, full of energy to have a love interest amidst pain and sorrow. It's uplifting and exciting.

"Joy comes, grief goes, we know not how" (James Lowell).

NO matter how your heart is broken the world doesn't stop for your grief and no matter how many friends you have, if you are their pillar, you will feel lonely and lost at the times you need them most, so "be strong in the lord and his mighty power to heal" (Ephesians 6:10).

"For he shall give his angels charge over you, to keep you in all your ways" (Psalm 91:11).

"A gentle word is never lost…. It cheers the heart when sorrow-tossed, and lulls the cares that bruises it" (Hastings).

We see those we love in every sunrise and in every sunset, in every tree and in every flower.

"Love, no greater theme can be emphasized; no stronger message can be proclaimed; no finer song can be sung; no better truth can be imagined" (Charles Swindoll).

To want love will block the way. You MUST love all. You must love or you cannot dwell in the house of the lord. Jesus says if you practice love He will bless you exceedingly above all. Leave it all to him. Peace will come. Trust.

God's love touches us each day with the glory of the morning sun, the laughter of a child, a drop of rain, the changing of the leaves.

If a care is too small to be turned into a prayer, it is too small to be made into a burden.

I have learned that you should always leave loved ones with loving words. It may be the last time you see them, because I believe sometimes the people you care about most in life are taken from you too soon.

Love has many forms, many pains, and sacrifice is one of them.

Love simply IS!

I've learned that no matter how you slice it, there will always be two sides.

The way children react. They could be laughing one minute and then cry the next. How nice it is – they live truly by the minute and seize that moment with their purity.

I ask God every day to take away the pain in my heart – to unbreak my heart – and he gives me that wish by granting me those precious little gifts – my children, the snowfall, laughter, and love.

Love is nothing unless we give it away.

Love is a willow tree bending in the wind, but not breaking.

When that first cry you hear of a baby being born you think – well little one, that won't be the first time you're scared. Your life is just beginning. You don't know the future. Who knows if you will remember the past, but right now here you are.

Healing to me occurs as you admit to yourself that a higher power than you is in control and there isn't a darn thing you can do, so you go on because YOU can control that!